SAVE THE DOLPHINS

SAVE THE DOLPHINS

Horace E. Dobbs B.Sc. Ph.D.

Foreword by
H R H The Duke of Edinburgh K.G., K.T.,
International President of the World Wildlife Fund

SOUVENIR PRESS

To Kay whose zest for life
and spirit of freedom took her on a
sailing voyage deep into the Pacific
Ocean from which she never returned.

First published 1981 by Souvenir Press Ltd,
43 Great Russell Street, London WC1B 3PA
and simultaneously in Canada

ISBN 0 285 62437 7

Filmset by Northumberland Press Ltd,
Gateshead, Tyne and Wear
Printed in Great Britain by
Richard Clay (The Chaucer Press) Ltd, Bungay, Suffolk

FOREWORD

Two things are required to achieve the conservation of endangered species; scientific facts about the life-cycle, habitat and the threats to its survival, and secondly, the will to introduce appropriate conservation measures. The former depends on objective study, the latter depends on propaganda and the stirring of human emotions. The author has used all his intricate knowledge of dolphins for the latter purpose and in so doing, I believe that he has made a most valuable contribution to the conservation of a particularly attractive species of wild animal.

Buckingham Palace,
July 1981

'For now is all the time there may be'

Inscription under the bronze sculpture of dolphins
which also serves as a sundial outside the National
Maritime Museum, Greenwich.

ACKNOWLEDGEMENTS

This book is not just my story and the photographs were not all taken by me. It has been compiled from a mass of tales and pictures from a great variety of sources. I am pleased to acknowledge all of those who have so willingly provided me with material. It would be virtually impossible to detail all of you by name. I hope, therefore, that those of you who read this and are not listed below will be able to identify yourselves and will accept a very sincere thank you from me.

Of those with whom I have corresponded I feel I must offer special thanks to John Denzler, notably for permission to reprint his article 'A Strange Encounter' which appeared in *Yachting Monthly*. The *Daily Mail* are also thanked for allowing me to quote extensively from John Edwards' report on the dolphin slaughter at Iki. The pictures used to illustrate this tragic story were taken at considerable risk by Suzie Cate of Greenpeace and reached me via Hardy Jones of the Living Ocean Society and Glenn Chase of The Fund for Animals in Washington.

I thank Gordon Ridley for telling me of his experiences in the Faroe Islands and for allowing me to choose from his excellent collection of photographs.

Chris McLoughlin kindly presented me with a selection of photographs of Sandy, the dolphin who became his special friend, and my thanks also go to Pat Selby who gave me a greater insight into the character of the elusive dolphin.

The photograph of Anne Rennie was provided by the *Eastern Province Herald*, Port Elizabeth.

Barry Wills, D. J. Nunn, Mrs Skinner, John Pile and Norman Cole all kindly provided me with pictures of our mutual friend Donald, and numerous people have written to me telling me of their encounters with this mischievous dolphin. Doug Godwin did the art work for the figure illustrating Donald's Odyssey and Doug's expertise in the darkroom is reflected in many of the black and white photographs in this book.

I have also to thank my correspondents in far away New Zealand for telling me of the exploits of my namesake, Horace, and for the considerable efforts they made to send me illustrations. They include Quentin Bennett, Frank Robson and Ros Rowe. I also thank Margaret Bingham for her touching poem.

The indefatigable Estelle Myers, the Australian Director of Project Interlock, took the picture of the founder of the Interlock project—Wade Doak—with whom I have developed a bond despite the fact that he lives half-way round the world from England. Wade's own story is told in his book called *Dolphin, Dolphin.*

My filming partner Chris Goosen, a person of incredible drive and energy, never gave up hope in our hunt for the elusive dolphin in the Red Sea. Without his involvement I would never have met another friendly wild dolphin under the sea.

I also gratefully acknowledge the help I have had from my family—wife Wendy and children Melanie and Ashley without whose unswerving support I would not have been able to champion the cause of the dolphins.

Finally, I thank Kerry Davis for transcribing my tapes and embarrassingly untidy scrawl into a typed manuscript.

H.E.D.

CONTENTS

Foreword by H R H The Duke of Edinburgh   5

Acknowledgements   7

Preface   11

1   Happy Reunions   13

2   Messing About With Boats   28

3   Sandy   55

4   Horace in New Zealand   65

5   International Dolphin Watch   74

6   Take me to the Dolphins   90

7   Death on the Beach   96

8   Hunt the Dolphin   103

9   Undersea Railroad   118

PREFACE

Those who have read *Follow a Wild Dolphin* will understand why I have written this book. In that book I described the joy of diving with a wild dolphin in the sea and the profound effect my experiences with Donald the dolphin had upon me.

Our friendship started off an island famous for its motorcycle TT races and cats without tails—the Isle of Man. It continued as the dolphin set out on an odyssey that was to cause me to meet him again off the coast of Wales and yet again in the sea off England's most westerly extremity—Cornwall.

Almost everyone who encountered Donald felt joy from the experience. Many fell in love with him despite, or perhaps because of, the fact that wherever he went his mischievous antics caused havoc amongst some of those upon whom he bestowed his attentions. In doing so he courted disaster at the hands of man and cheated death many times. Donald left a trail of broken hearts as he journeyed around the coast of Britain.

I make no secret of the fact that I too was caught in his magic web. At the end of *Follow a Wild Dolphin*, I left Donald—cavalier as ever—becoming a film star off the picturesque fishing village of St. Ives in Cornwall.

'What happened to him?' is the first question I am invariably asked by those who followed the saga of Donald. Thus, one reason for writing this book is to pick up some of the threads of Donald's life and so answer this question.

I had hoped to be able to round off the tale of Donald with a 'Happy ever after' ending. But I sadly regret I have not been able to do so.

Another reason for writing this book was that, at the time Donald was cavorting around Britain and bringing pleasure to millions, storm-clouds were gathering over the dolphin populations throughout the world. To the west, countless numbers of dolphins were being killed in the tuna fishing industry. In the east, dolphins were being treated as criminals and hunted down and butchered by the Japanese. Added to this, there was the enigma of dolphins destroying themselves by becoming stranded.

In addition to the obvious effects of these circumstances on dolphin populations, there was evidence to suggest that they were also under threat from other, more sinister enemies; the insidious effects of heavy metals and pesticides in the sea. Even sonic pollution was taking its toll.

I had to do something.

In presentations on radio and television, and in lectures throughout the world, I vehemently denounced the decimation of all cetaceans. At the same time I tried to explain my conviction that there is something very special between man and dolphin that transcends all other human–animal friendships. As a scientist brought up in the traditional strict disciplines of mathematics, physics and chemistry I would not have been surprised if this proposal had been received with scepticism, if not ridicule, by my peers. But this was not so. Some of the people I spoke to said they too felt a very strong affinity with dolphins but could not explain why.

As a researcher who had worked in the fields of human and veterinary medicine I was also able to propound my views to groups of highly qualified physicians and veterinary surgeons. When I did so there was general agreement that there was something special in the psyche of dolphins that affected many people. Those who had come into close contact with cetaceans agreed that dolphins had a mysterious quality—a kind of magic—that was in some way uplifting. They felt better people from the experience.

Against this background the news that dolphin populations were being depleted at an alarming rate was received with horror. Our discussions raised the even broader issues of 'What kind of world do I want to live in?' and 'What kind of world do I want to leave behind for my grandchildren to inherit?' These questions were posed in the sure knowledge that once the last of a species of any whale was dead no miracle of evolution would bring it back on the earth again.

I would not be so presumptuous as to proffer solutions to these major problems. However, as dolphins cannot speak for themselves, I can act as their advocate.

In this book, therefore, I have set out to establish the existence and the nature of the special bond between man and dolphins, and to expose the plight in which entire populations of dolphins now find themselves.

I hope I will cause you, dear reader, at least to ponder on this problem and its broader issues. For there is a chance, just a chance, that by adopting the right attitudes and taking the steps necessary to save the dolphins we will make the world a better place, in more ways than one.

H.E.D.
North Ferriby
1981

1 HAPPY REUNIONS

Donald the wild dolphin had disappeared, and we waited on the head-land, peering out to sea, hoping he would return. The air was still, and the sea, flat as a pool of mercury, reflected the pink-tinged clouds like a mirror, adding to the expanse of the evening sky. From afar we saw a large vessel approaching the bay. As it came nearer we were aware that it was being escorted by Donald.

To the dolphin, the mass of displaced water in front of the bows was like a stream which propelled him almost effortlessly. The forward moving water was not all progressing at the same speed. The dolphin used his sensitive skin to detect the subtle differences of flow and adjusted his posture accordingly, weaving back and forth in the bow wave. It was an

Being close to Donald when he leapt out of the water was awesome and exhilirating.

D. J. Nunn.

experience he had had many times in the past and one that he never ceased
to enjoy

The act of sensing pleasure generated within the dolphin an enzyme
with adrenalin-like properties which accumulated in his system. The
effect was like that of hauling a roller-coaster to the top of the run. He
could feel the energy building up inside his body and with it a sense of
expectation at the exhilaration to follow. Suddenly he was over the top.
The energy had to be released. With a few powerful sweeps of his tail he
accelerated ahead of the boat, headed towards the surface and gave one
all-mighty thrust that sent his body arching high out of the water.

For a few brief moments the dolphin enjoyed the sense of flying
through the air. Then came the delight of feeling the water smack his body
as he nosed head-first back into the sea. But the energy within him still
had a way to run. So he allowed his momentum to carry him down to the
seabed before turning sharply upwards. Again he thrashed with his tail as
hard as he possibly could and launched himself once more through the
silver interface between the water and the sky above it. Such was the
energy released, that the six hundred and fifty pound dolphin appeared to
fly effortlessly through the air. The red glow of the sun tinted his body
orange as it formed a fleeting silver archway over the flat, rose-hued sea.
Within seconds we had our boat launched and were heading out to sea.

After a lazy afternoon Donald was ready for his early evening frolic.
And he knew where the action would be next, for he recognised the noise
of our outboard engine. Without thinking, he swung his head towards the
sound and registered our position and speed. He started to swim, but not
directly towards us. His brain had already processed the information, and
with the rapidity of a computer indicated a direction which would bring
the dolphin and the rubber inflatable onto a collision course. As the gap
between us closed, the dolphin emitted a series of sound signals. Those
reflected by our hull enabled Donald to determine the range exactly. He
humped the water briefly to take a full breath of air. He changed course
slightly, accelerated to full speed in a few seconds, and headed straight for
us. Still maintaining course, Donald dived. Then with all of the power he
could muster he rushed headlong for the surface.

Like a Polaris missile he broke surface beside the inflatable.
Instinctively we ducked as the dolphin flew over our inflatable and
dropped headfirst into the water on the far side.

We were delighted to have Donald with us once again. Excitement in
the boat was building by the minute. Then the dolphin disappeared from
view.

We looked in all directions, because we knew from previous experience that he could appear anywhere within a range of 200 yards. Then one of us happened to glance down over the stern and under the ruffled water behind the boat could see a grey torpedo shape. Donald was back with the tip of his snout, or beak, just a few inches from the whirling propeller, enjoying the pulsating massage of the water thrust backwards over his streamlined body.

'He's here again,' shouted Nick excitedly, 'he's over the stern.'

'Right, let's get out the aquaplane. Ashley, you can go in first.'

The aquaplane consisted of a small rigid plastic board with metal handles on it. It was attached to the transom by about twenty yards of strong line.

When Ashley was towed behind the boat on an aquaplane the dolphin became very excited.
Horace Dobbs.

The boy slipped over the side of the now stationary inflatable and swam away from the stern carrying the aquaplane. The boat moved forward, and the line came taut. With his arms outstretched, Ashley held onto the handles and was hauled through the water. He was able to move in any direction behind the boat simply by deflecting the board. It is a remarkably simple yet effective device and the dolphin responded to it immediately. Thus Ashley had the double pleasure of the thrill of a tow, plus the even greater thrill of having the dolphin swimming alongside. But it was not only Ashley who appeared to be excited and enjoying the double dose of fun. The dolphin, who had spent many hours playing with the boy in the sea, also seemed to derive much greater pleasure when his human companion had an extra turn of speed and became slightly more dolphin-like in his aquatic capabilities. As Ashley dived and surfaced and zig-zagged from side to side the dolphin followed his every movement. Sometimes the dolphin would nudge Ashley's arm with his head, as if encouraging him to feats of even greater daring. When he looked at Donald beside him in the water Ashley could see the dolphin nodding his head vigorously up and down in a gesture which seemed to indicate his approval at the way in which the game was developing. As the game progressed the dolphin became more and more boisterous.

Like two unleashed dogs, whose sizes and capabilities were completely unmatched, Ashley and Donald cavorted one with another. Being able to out-perform his companion in every way the dolphin would sometimes rush ahead, swim round the inflatable, divert round one of the several boats moored in the bay and return to his human companion as if his tail was alight. We never knew what to expect next. Several times the dolphin took Ashley's outstretched arm or an ankle in his mouth and gave it a playful nip. It was a rough and tumble with plenty of physical contact.

After Ashley had climbed back into the boat we continued to tow the aquaplane behind the inflatable because Donald obviously enjoyed it. With no one clinging to it the aquaplane bounced over the surface.

The dolphin's attitude towards the aquaplane now became like that of a kitten towards a trailed piece of string. This similarity in behaviour was revealed when we discovered that sometimes Donald would disappear and remain hidden from view behind a moored Dory. When the inflatable next passed the Dory, the dolphin would rush out and leap high in the air. Once we had unravelled his tactics a new and exhilarating game developed. We would swing our craft with its trailing aquaplane deliberately close to the Dory, and Donald would charge across the surface towards us. Then the dolphin would dive. A few seconds later there would be a whoosh as Donald rocketed out of the sea.

We were in a pitch of excitement as Donald performed one leap after another. The dolphin too was in a highly excited state. Sometimes, between leaps, he would rub his abdomen vigorously against the keel of the Dory, causing it to rock violently.

Time lost all meaning. The sun set. And it was not until the light intensity had diminished and a quiet grey dusk settled on the sea that we became aware of the world again. It was as if for a time we had been alone with the dolphin in a capsule charged with an atmosphere of intense excitement. In our transparent bubble the spirits of three humans had reached the highest peaks in a rare and spontaneous union with a truly wild animal—a wild animal who was totally free and capable of bursting the bubble at any time simply by swimming away out of the bay.

As darkness descended and the inflatable nosed its way gently back to the shore, we realised for the first time that we had just participated in what must have been one of the most unique dolphin shows ever performed. During the course of the evening people had turned out of their hotels. The harbour wall and every other vantage point was lined with spectators. The crowd had enjoyed an unexpected evening of holiday entertainment and expressed their appreciation in the traditional manner. As we stepped ashore we were greeted with a round of enthusiastic applause.

A diver from Bromley, who had recognised me, came over. 'That was fantastic, 'Oris,' he said, 'at one time the dolphin came so low over yer 'ead I thought 'e'd knock yer 'at off.'

A boy rushed up to me and said, 'Are you training him, mister?'

A little old lady, too shy to speak to me directly, turned to my wife and commented rhetorically, 'You will thank your husband for that wonderful display, won't you?'

To which Wendy replied, 'It was Donald who put on the display, not my husband.'

The pub in the harbour at Coverack was packed to capacity. So we drove out of the fishing village to seek an alternative hostelry. Fortunately, like most other parts of rural Britain, the Lizard is well blessed with such establishments. We found an unpretentious but ideally suitable pub called The Three Tuns in St. Kevern. Carrying glasses of wine and plates bearing generous helpings of hot cheese and potato pie we made our way through the jostling crowd of predominantly young holidaymakers to a table in the secluded garden. As it was the last night of our visit the four of us discussed the exciting events of the past few hours and reviewed the entire situation of Donald and ourselves. For the wild dolphin had been directly responsible for bringing us all together at that point in time. Furthermore, Donald had brought about dramatic changes in all of our lives.

Had it not been for that solitary dolphin, who had chosen humans for company instead of his fellow dolphins, I would not have changed from a successful career in medical research to take up an exciting but precarious living as a freelance speaker, writer and broadcaster and self-styled delphinologist; my wife, Wendy, would not have resumed her professional career after seventeen years as a housewife; my son, Ashley,

would not have moved from the local comprehensive school to a boarding
school in Grimsby—a change which completely altered his attitudes to
education and gave him a much broader perspective of life; and finally our
companion, Nick Webb, would not have decided to sell almost everything
he possessed in order that he could spend the summer of 1977 closely
following a wild dolphin whose strange and eventful odyssey round the
British coast had started in 1972 off the Isle of Man, taken him to Wales
and had now brought him to one of the most spectacular and beautiful
parts of England.

The spectacular session with Donald was a fitting end to a holiday. Three
weeks earlier I had left my home in East Yorkshire and headed for
Cornwall knowing that by the normal laws of chance the possibility of
locating the dolphin was as remote as winning the football pools. But
inside me the fire of hope burned, fuelled by the knowledge that
several times in the past, despite equally enormous odds, I had made
contact with the dolphin and dived with him in the sea. I seemed to be
guided to him by a mysterious force which I could not explain. As I drove
into Falmouth, I wondered if the magic would still be there after nearly
a year.

I parked my car close to the harbour. I had stopped only once on the
nearly four hundred mile journey from home and I was stiff when I
climbed out of the driving seat. As I did so I felt an immediate compulsion
to walk to the harbour wall. I hurried to the jetty and joined a small knot
of four or five people who were watching some activity on the water about
thirty yards away. I did not speak to them but I knew instinctively why
they were there.

I looked towards a small boat tied to a mooring buoy. As I watched, I
saw a silver grey dome rise above the water. It moved slowly forward and
sank gently. A dark grey triangular fin quickly followed and moved
across the surface of the sea like a sail boat in a gentle breeze, leaving
behind a tiny wake on the grey green water. It slowly circled the moored
boat and then the head again humped the surface to take another breath
of air.

I stood on the jetty mesmerised by the sight of my dolphin. A feeling of
great joy built up inside me. I felt like waving and shouting out to Donald
'Hey Donald, I am here, I am here'. Had I been on my own I would
certainly have done so. However, the possibility that the other people
present may have thought I was an escapee from the local lunatic asylum,

prevented me from openly expressing my delight. Instead I remained silent and let the delight build up inside me like wine rapidly fermenting in a sealed bottle. As I stood there, finding it harder and harder to contain my joy, I realised that something else was building up inside me. I hurried away from the jetty.

When I returned, I was still in a mood of slight amazement, hardly daring to believe I had located Donald so easily. It was uncanny. In some mysterious way I had known where to go and when to be there. True, it was not a totally chance meeting, because I had taken advantage of whatever intelligence services I could tap. So from 'phone calls made before leaving home I knew Donald had been seen in the Falmouth area. But sightings showed that he frequently made excursions which took him from St. Ives to Fowey, a distance of about 100 miles. Furthermore, if I had been just one hundred yards away from the place where I felt compelled to look I certainly would not have found the dolphin. The first shot I had taken to locate him was a bullseye.

It was mid-evening, and despite the exultation I had experienced on seeing Donald again, I was tired and hungry. So I waved Donald a brief

Donald with a diver in Falmouth.

Barry Wills.

and silent farewell, hopeful that I would find him again the following day. I did so however, not knowing that Lady Luck had decided she had already bestowed upon me more than my fair share of good fortune. I set off to locate Dr. Nicholas Webb—a scientist who was spending his summer months studying Donald. Nick had dived with the dolphin several times and I was anxious to find out how his experiments were progressing.

I found Nick in the Globe Hotel where he had taken a part-time job as a barman and handyman.

Donald was nowhere to be seen when we later walked along the water's edge to look for the dolphin.

The following day was squally and there was no sign of Donald in Falmouth. Nick said that the dolphin sometimes made his way into the Helford River. So, as the temporary barman had agreed to meet a couple of his friends at the Ferry Boat Inn, we made our way there and parked on the beach. The car gave us a refuge from the wind and the rain showers and, at the same time, provided a vantage point from which to keep a look-out for Donald.

Nick and his two friends were highly entertaining company and Helston was a delightful place to pass the hours, but at no time did we see the flurry of activity in the river which would have heralded Donald's arrival. When he came onto the scene the dolphin always became a focus of attention. The ferryman welcomed the dolphin. Trade became very brisk because he took his small vessel to the dolphin to the delight of those onboard. If Donald made one of his spectacular leaps the passengers cheered and felt that they had had their money's worth. When we asked the boatman if he had seen the dolphin that day he replied that sadly Donald was not in the area. As an afterthought he added: 'If you find the dolphin, send him here. I could do with the extra business.'

On this occasion the reason for my presence in the West Country was to run an underwater photography course at the Underwater Centre at Fort Bovisand near Plymouth. I had to leave the following day without a further sighting of the dolphin. As I drove to my next destination I was heartened by the prospect that I had already made plans to return to Cornwall with my family. Next time I would have more time to spend renewing my acquaintance with Donald.

And so it was that two weeks later, with my wife Wendy and sixteen-year-old son Ashley in the car, I headed back towards Cornwall on what was for all of us a holiday with an objective—to find Donald the dolphin.

About two miles out of Falmouth I spotted Nick walking along the footpath. He climbed into the car and told us that Donald had not been seen for several days. We went to the jetty where I had seen him previously, but there was no sign of our mischievous friend. We decided that the only course of action was to set up a 'Hunt the Dolphin' operation. We drove to Helston, which was crowded with holidaymakers, but drew a blank there. In our investigations we talked to one lady who told us of a local headmaster who had taken out a group of children in kayaks. They had been intercepted by Donald who enjoyed himself and delighted the children by pushing them around, but she could not give us any information on recent sightings of the missing dolphin. At the end of the day we were no nearer our goal.

The next day was also devoted to reconnaissance. We contacted an ex-neighbour who had an office in Falmouth. It had a splendid seagull's eye view of the harbour and Jimmy Simpson regaled us with stories of Donald's antics as seen from his office window. One tale which he found particularly amusing involved a very smart and expensive German cruiser which came in to tie up to a mooring buoy. Apparently, just as a crew member on deck was about to snag the buoy rope with a boat hook, the buoy moved mysteriously away and out of reach. This caused some confusion onboard and the boat had to manoeuvre in the confined anchorage in order that the bows could be brought alongside the buoy once again. As the boat slowly approached the buoy and the boat hook was again lowered to fish for the line, the buoy moved away just out of reach. By this time Jimmy had called the other members of his staff into the office to watch the comedy routine taking place below. The memory of the incident was so clear in Jimmy's mind that he could only recount the story to us between bouts of laughter. For apparently those onboard the vessel did not take the incident very kindly and the man at the wheel started to scream at the crewman, chastising him for his blithering incompetence at not being able to carry out a simple task like hooking up the buoy.

Donald kept up the game of buoy pulling for a considerable time, much to the immense embarrassment of the captain and his crew and to the even greater amusement of those assembled in Jimmy's office. Eventually the submerged dolphin allowed the crewman to grab the buoy. However, just at the crucial moment, as the sailor was thankfully pulling it inboard, the dolphin gave the line a final tug. And only by a remarkable display of acrobatic agility did the luckless crew member manage to avoid going overboard to join the dolphin in the water.

When Jimmy had recovered from his own merriment, I was able to explain that the story he had just told us was typical of the dolphin's sense

Save the Dolphins

Donald was always ready for a game – but there were a few who did not find his antics amusing.

Barry Wills.

of humour. Donald appeared to take a special delight in disrupting the activities of serious-minded humans. By turning a routine procedure into a farce he demonstrated that there could be a lighter side to every situation. Was he showing us that humans might all enjoy life a little more if they did not take many of their activities quite so seriously? If that was his message, then I was receptive to it. We were on holiday and there was no point in spoiling it by becoming frustrated at not locating the dolphin. So we left the area to visit some other friends of Donald in the little fishing village of Mousehole near Penzance.

Those friends were Geoff and Liz Bold. Geoff, who was mechanic of the Penlee lifeboat, had studied Donald when the dolphin adopted the area outside the lifeboat station as one of his resting places. He told us that Donald had been seen in the Lizard region. Having enjoyed a pleasant afternoon in Mousehole we journeyed forth again and went to the tip of the Lizard, the southernmost headland in England. As we stood on that bleak and remote cliff top at sunset, we could see the sea stretching for miles about us in a huge unbroken arc which extended through three-quarters of a circle. On that vast expanse of sea a single dolphin would represent no more than a pin prick. So what chance did we really have of finding the elusive Donald? Was I trusting too much to the magic which had worked in the past?

The following morning, we met up again with Nick and were joined by two other friends who were keen to meet Donald for the first time. With three cars at our disposal we decided to go our separate ways, and to this day I do not know why I chose to go in the opposite direction to the others. I selected to go back onto the Lizard. Wendy and Ashley were with me and we eventually descended into Coverack, which I discovered to my delight complied with my romantic ideal of a secluded Cornish fishing village. At the heart was the tiny harbour. The tide was low and the boats lay heeled over in picturesque confusion. An old cannon, half buried in the sand, provided a post to which their algae-covered mooring chains were attached. I stopped the car and peered down over a stone wall to the harbour below. Some children were running gleefully in and out of the crystal clear water. There was a jumble of small boats directly beneath me. The water was about three feet deep and I noticed a white plastic rowing dinghy. Then to my unbounded joy I saw a dark silver-grey shape cruising slowly around the dinghy.

I don't think I had ever seen Donald looking so immaculate before. The bright sunlight, reflected from the pure yellow sand beneath him, illuminated his underside which seemed to shine as if it were solid silver. The silver underside merged with the dark-grey topside which had the appearance of burnished pewter. At that moment, Donald looked like a perfect dolphin, in a perfect setting, on a perfect sunny day.

A few minutes later I had donned my wetsuit. Wearing just fins, mask and snorkel, I finned rapidly towards the middle of the bay, for, during the time it had taken me to change, Donald had moved out of the harbour and I was anxious to make contact quickly just in case he decided to take off on another journey.

As I approached, I called out to him through my snorkel tube but he did not come to greet me. It was time for his mid-day rest and he was in no mood to play. When I reached him, I stroked him. He closed one eye and rolled over, inviting me to stroke his abdomen. We stayed together for about twenty minutes before I made my way back to shore. I knew from previous experience that Donald was seldom in high spirits in the middle of the day. I left him in peace, knowing that if he was undisturbed when he wanted to be alone, he was less likely to seek a more peaceful place elsewhere.

In the mid afternoon I again put on my wetsuit and headed out towards the middle of the bay. This time Donald came to meet me and the two of us enjoyed playing gently with one another. Through my snorkel tube, I spoke to Donald as I would have done to an old acquaintance after an absence of several months.

Then Donald moved away from me and I saw that he was making his way towards a lady wearing a bright red bathing cap who was swimming the breast stroke towards the middle of the bay. I finned towards them and when I reached her she was gently stroking the dolphin. Within a few minutes we were talking to one another over the back of the dolphin. She asked me about my past and Donald's past, as if we were conversing across a coffee table. I don't think for one moment that it struck her as at

Encounter with Donald.
Horace Dobbs.

all incongruous that we should hold such a discussion in the middle of a bay across the back of a dolphin whilst we were treading water. The lady spoke with a cultured voice and had an air of complete imperturbability. I felt she could have dealt with even the most bizarre situation without what in modern parlance would be termed 'losing her cool'. I did not know at the time that my assessment of her would be put to the test the following day.

It happened after I had taken tea with her and her mother in their house which overlooked the bay. Nick had joined us and our mid-morning tea break came to a natural conclusion when Donald made his appearance in the bay. We all decided it was time to pay him another visit.

The lady in the red bathing cap swam out from the shore, whilst the rest of us, younger, and less hardy individuals, donned our wetsuits to keep out the cold. We even used motorised transport in the form of Nick's inflatable to reach the middle of the bay. Getting kitted up and the preparation of the boat took several minutes. By the time we were ready for our encounter with Donald he was already circling the swimmer and was rubbing himself against her bare legs. I knew immediately from the manner in which he diverted and approached us at full speed that the dolphin was in a playful mood and we could be in for a boisterous romp. I was not disappointed. We took it in turns to leave the boat and go into the water with him. Meanwhile our lady swimmer continued to take her morning exercise, unperturbed by occasional visits from the dolphin and the antics that were going on around her.

When Donald is in one of his most energetic moods he is really awesome. And that morning there seemed to be no end to the energy he was prepared to expend.

When Ashley was in the water, the dolphin leapt high over him several times. The sight of six hundred and fifty pounds of dolphin soaring out of the water and then plummeting back into the sea at very close quarters left an image in my eyes that stayed for a few seconds after the event was over. It was frighteningly exciting because at the back of my mind lurked the knowledge that, despite all that had gone before, Donald was still a wild animal. In truth we knew very little about him. He could have killed us all in a few seconds if he chose—by ramming us with his beak as he might quickly dispose of a shark. However, I had no sense of aggressive feelings coming from him, and dismissed that possibility completely.

As Ashley climbed back into the inflatable I slipped overboard to join the dolphin in his world.

Dr. Nick Webb and I had had long discussions on dolphin behaviour and had debated in detail how we could study the dolphin. All of our proposed experiments depended upon Donald's voluntary co-operation and we both agreed that we would never try to confine the dolphin or attempt to fix instruments, such as radio transmitters, to him. We felt that to do so would disturb the relationship the dolphin had spontaneously established with us. Also, and of the utmost importance, was the fact that it would be contrary to the spirit of freedom which the dolphin somehow symbolised to both of us. When I took to the water that morning all thoughts of testing the dolphin vanished from my mind. It was as if I was overwhelmed completely by the spirit of the dolphin who just wanted to play and enjoy himself. If ever any animal radiated a sense of joy and sheer pleasure at being alive and free, then Donald did so in full measure that morning.

When Donald came alongside me and we had exchanged our usual greetings, I cupped my two hands round the front of his dorsal fin. The result could not have been more exciting if I had been mounted on a racehorse and the starting gates suddenly opened. Donald rushed forward at full speed across the surface of the sea with me clinging to him as if my very life depended upon it. The sea swirled up between my arms and foam cascaded over my shoulders. The rushing water partially obscured the vision through my facemask which was just above the water. Being so close to the surface, the sensation of speed was heightened. Ahead of me I could see clear water. Occasionally this view was broken by the brief appearance of the shining dome of Donald's head as he took a rapid breath.

Fish eye views of Donald the dolphin and Ashley Dobbs playing together beneath the sea.

Horace Dobbs.

I could always have left my metaphorical mount merely by letting go of the dolphin's dorsal fin, but it was Donald who decided when it was time for my joyride to end. He simply rolled to one side. This caused his fin to slip from my grasp.

I once again realised how inadequate were my own swimming capabilities when Donald deliberately broke my connection with him and accelerated away to give the rubber inflatable a playful swipe with his tail.

After one particularly thrilling tow, I climbed back into the inflatable and Donald turned his attention to the lady who was still swimming steadily doing the breast stroke in the middle of the bay. All of a sudden Donald dived and came up underneath her, lifting her bodily out of the water. Like a sack of potatoes tossed onto the back of a horse she was draped helplessly over his neck region. She was prevented from slipping off backwards by his dorsal fin as he accelerated forwards. With his new passenger onboard Donald rushed at full speed towards the inflatable as if to show off his prowess as a racing sea horse. Indeed, I would not have been surprised if he had tried the role of a steeplechaser and attempted to jump right over the inflatable with his astounded jockey still on top.

Instead, he decided it was the flat racing season, and he followed a course which took him past the inflatable with a tremendous flurry of water caused by his trailing load.

It was at this stage that I realised what it is in the British character that separates some of us from the rest of Europeans, especially the Latins. Can you imagine what a highly excitable Italian lady would have done in the circumstances? I leave that to you.

Completely unperturbed, but obviously very much surprised at finding herself hurtling across the bay on the back of the dolphin, the lady in the swimsuit and the red bathing cap managed to gasp in her refined crisp English accent as she raced past the inflatable, 'Is this usual behaviour?'

She was gone before I could reply. As my answer would have been an emphatic 'No', for I had never before seen Donald behave in such a manner towards a swimmer, we hastened after her at full speed to render whatever assistance might be required.

We caught up with her when Donald eventually decided it was time for a different game. I invited her to climb aboard the inflatable just in case the dolphin decided to practise any more of his outrageous behaviour. But as it turned out I was much more anxious for her safety than she appeared to be.

When we got back to the lifeboat slipway, I was cold from my immersion in the sea, despite the fact that I was wearing a wetsuit. Our swimmer friend, who did not have the benefit of any neoprene insulation, rubbed herself down, and with her large bath towel wrapped around her, made her way back to her mother's house. As she departed I had nothing but admiration for her stamina and stoicism.

2 MESSING ABOUT WITH BOATS

Ever since I first met Donald I have tried to find out as much as I can about him. Piecing together his past has proved to be a fascinating exercise which has revealed hidden and surprising stories of his relationship with man. The last sighting I obtained of Donald on the Isle of Man was 18 March 1975. When he turned up out of the blue beside my diving boat in August 1975 I was overjoyed to re-establish contact with him and local detective work showed that unbeknown to me he had been in the area for some time.

The first recorded sighting was on 5 April 1975, when in snow and windy weather a Bottlenosed dolphin was reported to have followed the vessel *Sharan*, a converted lifeboat, from Milford Haven to the island of Skomer. The *Sharan* was towing a small clinker-built wooden pram dinghy, which appeared to be the main attraction for the dolphin.

Subsequently the dolphin formed a strong association with the dinghy and his behaviour was observed and recorded by Pembrokeshire Parks Warden, Malcolm Cullen. The warden would ferry birdwatchers from the mainland to the islands of Skokholm and Skomer in the converted lifeboat which was kept moored in Martin's Haven during the summer months.

Donald soon discovered that the warden was a sympathetic person whose regular activities could provide a source of amusement. The dolphin would often spend the night in the haven resting alongside one of the moored vessels. He would greet the boatman when he came down to the beach early in the morning and often swam alongside the tender when it was sculled out to the *Sharan*. The dolphin liked the sounds of the big boat being prepared for the outward journey. He would swim excitedly around the bay when the visitors scrambled aboard, knowing that he would be undertaking his self-imposed escort duty to see the *Sharan* safely out of the bay. Sometimes he would swim with his beak just a few inches from the steadily revolving propeller. At other times he would ride the bows. Occasionally he would show his pleasure by jumping close to the vessel. If he succeeded in drenching the occupants of the boat with the splash so that they shrieked with surprise, he would swim alongside with his head out of the water to view with a mischievous eye the consternation he had caused onboard.

It was during his stay off Martin's Haven that Donald discovered a new trick that could cause a great deal of human confusion if it was done without anybody knowing of his presence. He would swim underneath a boat underway and exhale under the propeller. As the air bubble rose the blades of the propeller would have nothing to bite into. This absence of water resistance would cause the engine to increase its revolutions dramatically. As soon as the air had passed, the engine would resume its

Donald with the tender to the *Sharan* in Martin's Haven

John Pile.

normal speed. The unsuspecting helmsman would wonder what was happening. If he was quick enough he would slam the engine control down to low throttle as soon as the engine raced. When he brought it up to speed again all would be normal and he would puzzle over the reason for the sudden cavitation of the propeller.

If Donald was in a particularly mischievous mood he would play his trick two or three times without surfacing and, when he did eventually make his presence known, some boatmen did not connect the two incidents. Indeed, I suspect there are people still puzzling over the mysterious misbehaviour of the engines when they were in or near Martin's Haven. I am not sure which situations Donald relished the more: those in which his activity remained undiscovered and he made the machine appear to be master of the man, or when his prank was discovered, the fist waving and general exclamations hurled in his direction. For a dolphin who liked to be noticed at times, he certainly commanded an audience—albeit they were not demanding an encore performance.

Donald travelling at speed.   *Nick Baker.*

I had always assumed, following the use of underwater explosives to improve the harbour at Port St Mary in the Isle of Man, that Donald travelled straight to Wales. But this simple journey came into question when an article in *Yachting Monthly* was brought to my attention by Ruth Wharram—a lady who had led a very adventurous life as a sailor onboard Polynesian-style catamarans and who had a passion for dolphins. This is the article Ruth sent me which was entitled 'Strange Meeting'.

Securing the ketch to the mooring buoy had become a routine. The shipping forecast from the BBC had predicted severe gales for the Irish Sea and in anticipation of this "lazy" easterly, early in the day the skipper had decided to change the comfortable mooring alongside the jetty of the Royal Irish Yacht Club of Dun Laoghaire for the more lively offshore buoy. The Irish call that type of easterly a lazy wind because it doesn't bother to blow around you. It cuts right through you, especially in January.

The skipper had placed himself with the boat hook in the pulpit, aiming with the hook like an ancient whaler for the small loop which would secure the ketch to the buoy. His son was coiling lines and stowing them under the cockpit seats for the next landfall. I was handling the helm, keeping the bow end in the teeth of the stiff gusts, engine ticking over steadily. As a result of the daily exercise we accomplished this manoeuvre as a rule in one straight approach with a minimum of fuss. Thus, I needed a few open-mouthed seconds to find my voice in the clamour of the rigging as I suddenly sighted a large, shiny, rotating rubber tube a short distance ahead off the starboard bow. This tube, however, sprouted an impressive dorsal fin and knowing enough about tyre research I yelled, "A whale, starboard, a whale." In hindsight I know that the call "Thar she blows" would have been proper, but I challenge anybody to remember these nautical terms on the approach of a self-propelled rubber tube which by that time had flared out into a wide expanse of horizontal tail flippers, not unlike diving planes of a nuclear submarine. The beast went into a rolling dive to disappear underneath our sharp clipper bow, and the skipper at last caught my attention due to the deluge of icy Irish Sea which the downthrust of those flippers delivered to his face. His comments were mercifully and literally drowned.

Meanwhile, back at the helm I kept track of the direction and, sure enough, in the extended line of its course about 100 feet off to port a big clown's face jumped out of the waves, grinning and standing vertically in the water like a sales promotion for Cousteau's films. The whale had shrunk to become a bottlenosed dolphin. Mind you, it was still big, about 10–12 feet, but it was not a whale. It kept looking in our direction for a few seconds and renewed its dummy torpedo run. By now the skipper had singlehandedly secured the boat—a deed which proved our lingering suspicion that he never needed our help in the first place. We all yelled for a camera. However, his son and I being rather accomplished photographers succeeded in justifying the old adage once again: a Nikon remains at home when an Instamatic cannot handle the job. Perhaps a snapshot exists, but my later inquiries regarding results and possible copies, met with glaring looks. Therefore a sketch is offered instead.

While the battle of the picture was going on I went below to plug a cassette into our stereo system. We had a wide selection of popular classics, from Mozart's Piano Concerto, Vivaldi and Bach to Handel's Water Music. The dolphin received the full treatment of canned Karajan and the ferrocement hull must have provided a good resonating body. In any case, the first notes had barely penetrated the hull as the beast came alongside, inspecting the boat from stern to stem, frequently raising itself on its tail to create on deck a disturbing eyeball to eyeball confrontation between dripping dolphin and trembling deckhands. Our mounting excitement—a mixture difficult to define of delight and eery unease—quenched any thought of work. The encounter was to us obviously an attempt at contact, of communication by another intelligence that in our talks the comparison emerged of astronauts facing for the first time something as curious, as playful and perhaps as intelligent as man. During these contemplations the dolphin discovered our dinghy which had been streaming about 30 feet astern. It was one of those glassfibre, unsinkable tenders, vaguely following the lines of a catamaran. It was quite apparent that the dolphin was intrigued by this pushable, movable, bouncing entity and the beast coaxed it any which way it pleased and as far as the painter would

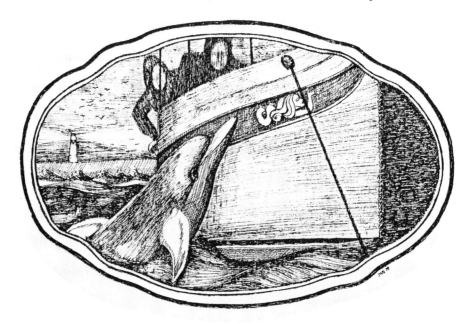

John Denzler's drawing of the incident in Dun Laoghaire.

permit. It dived underneath and started to lift it gently off the surface. This gave me time to appreciate the relatively safe decks of the ketch and I fervently prayed that all stories about the dolphin's life-saving capabilities were true. It happens that I cannot swim. It further happens that in January, in Dun Laoghaire, it wouldn't have made much difference. That, however, only occurred to me later.

Finally, the dolphin started to lose its patience with this placid, unresponsive item of orange plastic and it endeavoured to take a very close look inside which appeared as an attempt to board it. Discovering the hollow nature of the dinghy the dolphin lost all interest in it as a plaything and we became again the object of his attention. Observing its antics we realised that the beast was male, whereupon we asked ourselves if its behaviour could be attributed to a slightly confused mating ritual, and felt rather sorry for him. From the point of technical improvement we wished him all the luck with the dinghy. There is no doubt that a dolphin could have greatly improved the seagoing capabilities of that thing which daily challenged the depths of our collective courage, during the transfers from boat to shore. However, I remembered that sexual behaviour among various higher species frequently passes as a social contact or communication without reproductive objectives. We also considered Holy Loch and the alleged killer dolphins of the US Nuclear Submarine Fleet. If our dolphin was AWOL then we may have got a glimpse of the defensive tactics the dolphins use against enemy divers.

Meanwhile, the dolphin had become quite used to us and the music was still playing. He came alongside, rolling lazily over on his side to get a good look at the peering faces staring at him from the deck above. I reached down and started to scratch him on the underside of the flipper which seemed to please him for a while; at least, he didn't bite my hand off. However, our frustration had been mounting (never mind his). In spite of icy, frigid sea and wind we were greatly tempted to roll over the side and follow the beast into his mysterious and sheer endless realms. That included me who would have had some problem to get back to the surface. We were irritated that we lacked the capability to communicate, to exchange mutually meaningful information. Obviously, the animal had searched us out (there were about two dozen other vessels in port); he didn't mind hanging around and may even have had some fun. From a wild, untamed creature this is a unique and exhilarating behaviour. We racked our brains to develop some interchange and his continuously observing, occasionally blinking eye urged us on, but with the exception of the musical programme no great ideas emerged. Feeding was out of the question because we didn't know the right diet and worse, it brought the zoo comparison too close for comfort—with reversed roles. We were so apparently in the cage while he kept circling around us, observing, studying and trying to entice us to some entertaining behaviour. Perhaps I am reading too much into the incident but the creature certainly knew how to make us feel uneasy by injecting an icy, sobering dose of humility into our attitudes.

The afternoon turned into early evening and twilight and the dreaded moment to enter the dinghy to get ashore could not be avoided any longer. Without really becoming aware of it we suddenly realised that the dolphin had kept us enthralled for six solid hours, letting us forget chores and "chow". It began to dawn on my generally suspicious mind that the dolphin may have been savouring this moment as the grand finale all afternoon, waiting for us to get into that unstable contraption. Hurriedly I gave last-minute instructions in case we had completely misinterpreted the dolphin's behaviour and he was actually gleefully waiting to balance the score for the slaughter of his cousins, the whales. How do you explain to a dolphin that you are neither Japanese nor Soviet and in my particular case even neutral, a Swiss who shouldn't be on the water in the first place?

With the three of us concentrating on the whereabouts of the dolphin, we were truly lucky to secure a foothold in the dinghy at all. The heaving stern was of no assistance either. The skipper handled the oars while I kept a lookout in the stern and his son in the bow. By that time the wind had pushed us far enough from the ketch that in imitation of our Lord and Saviour for reasons of distance ceased to be a subject for contemplation. With perfect timing the beast picked this moment to take a bearing on us, throw himself into one of his easy, rolling dives and send my mind into a litany. "Oh, no, he wouldn't. Not with me in the dinghy. No."

Well, he didn't, but the skipper got another well-aimed soaking. The rest of us hollered and laughed. This brought the beastie back to the boat so that we all could pet him for a few seconds. By now, he had discovered the oars and their rhythmic movement greatly intrigued him. Unfortunately, it completely threw the skipper off his stroke and our course looked as if his son or I were handling the oars. Eventually we reached the boat launching ramp and waded ashore. The dolphin remained with us until it must have touched the concrete ramp. We kept telling him to turn around and head out for sea and another ship

which would take him into warmer waters. A few times he reared out of
the water pedalling on his powerful tail flippers, but since none of us
made any attempt to return to the boat he finally turned and
disappeared with that elegant, economical, slow roll in the wintry
whitecaps of Dun Laoghaire harbour.

Jimmy, the old seadog who is boatman at the Royal Irish, told us
that it was a lucky ship which got a dolphin's attention. Well, I
wouldn't know about that but I certainly felt lucky having experienced
this encounter, because, ever since, I have had spells of musing about
our presumptuous premises, man's supremacy in the animal kingdom.
We assume that a high intelligence will manifest itself in cultural
achievements. I suspect the opposite might be more conceivable: a truly
great intelligence who finds infinite adventures within its neurological
system and no compulsion to express any of it. An imagination so
highly evolved that he finds no need to implement action nor prove a
point. A being, free to roam the greatest inner space and at the same
time outer space—the sea on earth. A strange intelligence indeed.

I was very intrigued by John Denzler's scholarly and amusing article. The
last sentences admirably expressed my own thoughts about the dolphin's
use of its highly-evolved brain. However, there were aspects of his
encounter at Dun Laoghaire which seemed to indicate that the 'beast' to
which he referred was none other than my friend Donald. But was it? I
had two files full of Donald sightings. The article was published in 1978
and, during the previous winter, Donald was in Falmouth. So the actual
date of John Denzler's strange meeting was crucial.

With the aid of Ruth Wharram, I wrote to John Denzler and sent him a
copy of *Follow a Wild Dolphin* the existence of which he knew nothing
about. I received a letter by return which pinpointed the encounter to the
first three weeks in March 1975. As evidence John enclosed a photocopy
of the appropriate page of his passport which bore the date stamps for his
entry into Ireland and his next port of call—New York. The latter date
(23 March 1975) fitted exactly with a blank in sightings of Donald
between his departure from the Isle of Man and his arrival off the coast of
Wales.

However, I felt no self-respecting detective would base a case on a
single well-established clue. So I asked for more information.

The size of John Denzler's dolphin was about right.

John offered another reason to support the case for it being Donald. He
wrote: '. . . his behaviour was another clue to his identity . . . More than

once I felt—Jesus, I know this dude; it must be Donald. The way he ogled the inside of the dinghy was exactly your description of his fooling the Jack Russell.'

John Denzler did not confine his writing to factual matters only. He speculated that the dolphin may have followed the ferry into Dun Laoghaire. He suggested that dolphins, like humans, may drown themselves in brain stimulating activity: drugs, music, drink, colours, work, physical exertion to ease off painful memories. Thus Donald may have found relief from the memories of the explosion by immersing himself in the cacophony of sound coming from the large vessel.

He also commented on the Greek roots of the word Delphi '... which stands for whole, entire, unfractured, total. When you put this in context with the oracle's motto "Know thyself" I get this curious feeling again of an underlying purpose and meaning, a pattern which is more felt than seen, a connecting web of inter-species' communication and intelligence.'

His letter concluded: 'Finally, as a whimsical ending I would like to return to the first sentence of your book: "On 26 March ..." It happened to be my birthday and in 1972 when Henry Crellin met Donald I happened to be sailing in Greece near Delphi. I know perfectly well that there is no significance in such coincidental dates. It is just another of those zephyr touches which seem to surround dolphins and whales and some humans. It also made me feel when I started your book: this book is for me especially. Well it was and it is. Donald made another link after five years, the web is getting a bit stronger as well. Perhaps that's another example how dolphins manipulate man for their own purpose: to build a safety net for themselves by picking those humans who are sensitive to their needs ...'

Donald affected the lives of many humans who entered his orbit. The changes in their thoughts and activities he brought about, directly or indirectly, fascinated me. John Denzler, however, appeared to be extra special. I was so intrigued by his experiences and thoughts that I wanted to find out more about the man. When I enquired he answered with typical frankness. 'When I met Donald I had quit a career as art director for a first-rate international advertising agency. I was in a personal crisis and felt I couldn't go on anymore with this highly paid daily rubbish. My exit from the ad world had been rather dramatic. I virtually flung my loaded out-tray at the head of the chairman of the board.'

After he left Switzerland he drifted from Europe to America and back to Ireland where he carved the figurehead, bow scrolls and large sternboard for a ketch. In contrast to the contrived art of the advertising agency, John Denzler found the satisfaction and peace of mind he was searching for. 'I was in a trance, forgetting frequently food and rest, during this fantastic period of designing and carving these pieces.' It was just after he finished this work that he met Donald.

When all of the evidence was taken into account there was no doubt in my mind that the dolphin with whom John Denzler had his so-called 'strange encounter' was the one and only Donald.

Perhaps in some mysterious way the dolphin was drawn to John Denzler who had the distinct feeling that Donald was trying to communicate with him. The ad man who took to woodcarving tried hard to respond, but felt frustrated by his inability to do so. In one of his letters he referred to the subject of communication in human relationships. 'The discrepancy between the wealth of what we would like to communicate and what we actually can convey in words is the "human condition"—paradise lost.' It is this insufficiency that stimulates painters, drives poets and compels sculptors. 'And perhaps, the attraction some of us experience with dolphins stems from the "certainty" that they still live—as the ancients—with more complete modes of communication, with different channels.'

At the end of one of his letters John Denzler said he looked forward to further exchanges of ideas and that my letters had an uncanny knack of perfect timing. 'In any case,' he stated, 'they add a different dimension to my life: a touch of the sea in a stone desert.'

For my part, it was a joy to receive letters with such a poetic turn of phrase from somebody who was obviously a fellow spirit. John Denzler added a new and previously unknown leg to the picture I had built-up of Donald's odyssey around Britain.

When doing so he confirmed once again that there was something special, yet still intangible, in the relationships between humans and dolphins.

John Denzler's so-called 'Strange Meeting' was the only incident I uncovered about Donald's diversion to Ireland on his passage to Wales. However, I collected more stories about Donald's antics when he reached his new destination. One person who regaled me with first-hand accounts was John Davies.

I met John in Liverpool, at the historic Vines Hotel. It was an appropriate venue because the crowded room in which we sat was a place where countless stories had been exchanged over pints of frothy ale. John

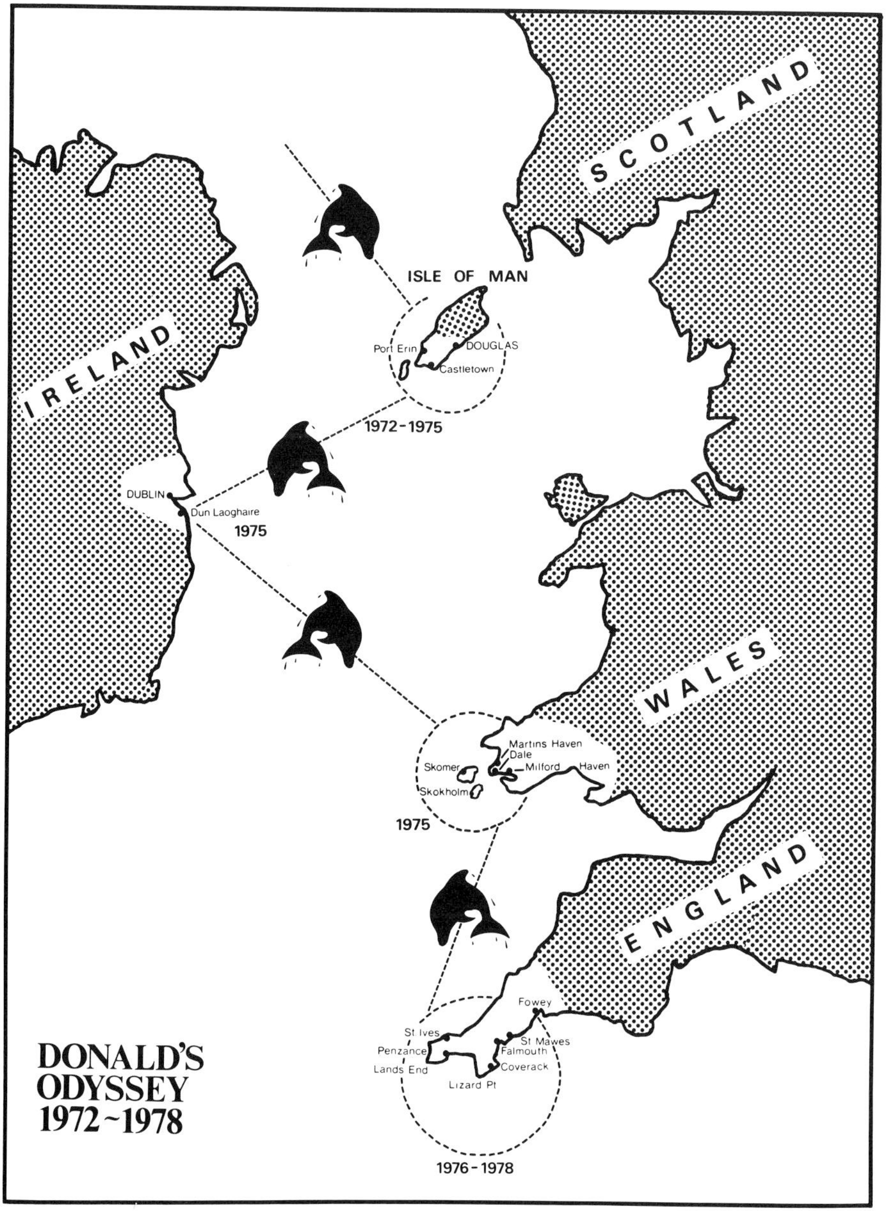

SCOTLAND

IRELAND

ISLE OF MAN

Port Erin   DOUGLAS

Castletown

1972-1975

DUBLIN

Dun Laoghaire

1975

WALES

Martins Haven
Dale
Skomer   Milford   Haven
Skokholm

1975

ENGLAND

Fowey

St Ives   St Mawes

Penzance   Falmouth

Lands End   Coverack

Lizard Pt

1976-1978

**DONALD'S
ODYSSEY
1972~1978**

had long dark hair, a beard, bright eyes and wore a grey roll-neck fisherman's sweater. He had a droll sense of humour, and I had to listen carefully to the tales he had to tell because he was quietly spoken. We met in Liverpool—the city where John was studying to become a town planner. However, the events which he recounted took place near his home town of Haverfordwest in Pembrokeshire.

In the summer season of 1975 John owned a rather old 505 dinghy—a boat which he described as having 'razor sharp responses, extreme manoeuvrability and generally sweet handling'. One evening when John was sailing back to the Yacht Club with a gentle steady breeze, Donald appeared between the dinghy and the slipway. Shortly afterwards the dolphin surfaced astern and then overtook the 505 at tremendous speed. Close to the stern he dived. As he did so John banged the helm down and was almost instantly going back the way he came.

'Donald surfaced quite a long way away, and I think looking a little unsure. So that he wouldn't feel rejected, I set course towards him,' continued John.

'What followed was one of the most astonishing things I have ever seen.'

Donald started his display by charging under the boat from the starboard side. John looked over the port side expecting to see the dolphin surface. But the dolphin did not appear. Instead he heard a splashing on the starboard side.

'Donald had doubled back under us and come up to starboard, obviously to say "I can do a U turn too!"'

John continued his story excitedly. 'After that for openers, he swam round us. Zig-zagged under us. Dived. Leaped. Well we did our best—and a 505 is good—but for speed, manoeuvrability, grace and flamboyance he had us totally outclassed.'

On summer evenings John would sometimes engage in point races in which different classes of dinghies would compete with one another.

'We would start five minutes after the GP14s, go screaming past them in a cloud of spray, then be a long way last on handicap. It was great fun, if hardly your deadly-serious dinghy racing ace image,' he explained laughing.

One blustery and grey evening John acted as crew on his own boat and had a very experienced sailor on the helm. The 505 was rocketing along in the stiff breeze and the sailors had to rivet their attention on the boat knowing that instant capsize was the penalty for a momentary lack of concentration. Then Donald decided it was time for a game. He swam over to the 505 and rushed through the water alongside in his own flurry of foam. When the crew ignored him he accelerated ahead. Finally the dolphin slipped back and followed astern, the tip of his beak just a few inches from the trailing edge of the rudder that was hissing through the water. Still getting no reaction from the crew, he took a playful swipe at the rudder with his tail and dived. There was a crack and the tiller went slack.

'I thought we were one for the rescue boat,' said John as he relived the incident.

A close encounter with Donald could be a memorable experience for those who messed about in small boats.

D. J. Nunn.

However, the helmsman managed to keep the boat upright and the dinghy changed course for home steering with the sails. The broken rudder was still attached to the boat, but flapping about in the water. The helmsman put his foot on the rudder to steady it and then announced that something was tickling his foot.

'It was of course Donald,' continued John indicating no animosity towards the playful dolphin he had ignored on that August evening.

'I'm sure he had taken a playful swipe at the rudder, and was now drawing our attention to his little joke.'

He continued the saga.

'Consider though, although the loss of steering had slowed us down, we were still going at a fair pace. And sheering around a bit—not to mention a bumpy little sea running. For Donald, following behind us that foot must have been gyrating about in a most unpredictable manner. It would have been easy to miss it—and not too hard to wallop it. But tickle it? What perfect control!'

Like many other people John Davies attributed human characteristics to Donald and he described him as 'A lovely fellow. Very pro-human, totally trustworthy, sometimes boisterous and sometimes subtle.'

It even occurred to John that Donald might be a dolphin ambassador to humanity.

Donald's 'I come in peace' approach, together with his intelligence and the lengths to which he would go to make people feel good, were, according to John, all factors which led him to think of the dolphin as a very special fellow inhabitant of our planet.

John Davies missed Donald when the dolphin set off for Cornwall. Before his departure, however, Donald left another story for the dinghy sailors of Dale to tell incredulous visitors to the Yacht Club, who did not have the benefit (or misfortune—depending upon your point of view) of a first-hand encounter with the mischief-making dolphin.

It happened on a summer's evening when the Club's GP14 dinghies were out on a points race. There was very little wind and the boats drifted lazily round the course, slowly sorting themselves into a line. The slowest helmsman started to lose interest in the race and decided simply to enjoy a lazy gentle cruise.

Sitting in the stern he let his hand trail in the water. All of a sudden he was surprised to feel something smooth touch his fingers. In startled surprise he pulled his hand out of the sea and looked down. To his amazement there was Donald's head like a grey shiny dome alongside his boat.

'Oh it's you Donald,' he said. 'What are you doing here?'

Donald raised his head out of the water and looked inside the dinghy.

The one-sided conversation with the dolphin continued with a rhetorical question.

'You OK then? I'm supposed to be racing. But there doesn't seem to be much point with so little wind, does there?'

At this point Donald nodded his head and with a mischievous glint in his eye disappeared beneath the surface.

'Well you didn't stay long did you?' the man continued, addressing his remark over the now empty water.

He sat back and continued to trail his hand in the sea. Then suddenly his dinghy started to gather speed. The helmsman immediately became alert and steered his boat past his nearest rival.

'This race could become interesting after all,' he said to himself, delighted with the turn of events.

He smiled to himself as he overtook his next rival who watched him pass with an expression of disbelief. With his competitive edge sharpened, the helmsman concentrated on making those fine adjustments that enable one person, a superior person, to sail a boat that much faster than the crew in another identical dinghy. With a growing feeling that he might gain some useful points, he urged his craft forward towards the next dinghy that would fall prey to his superior speed and sail.

Then gradually he lost way. He pulled at the sheet and pushed the tiller across but the dinghy would not respond. He was practically becalmed again. As he considered what to do next, there was a distinct sharp puff beside the boat and Donald's head broke surface. In the excitement of his newly acquired racing prowess the sailor had forgotten the dolphin.

'Phew Donald, you made me jump,' he exclaimed as Donald once again submerged.

The helmsman watched the indistinct grey torpedo shape move through the green brown water. It circled the boat just below the surface and came up to the stern. Then the sailor felt his boat surge forward once again. Donald was actually pushing the dinghy along.

'Well I'm damned,' blurted out the sailor as he suddenly became aware of the source of his newly acquired superiority.

'Keep it up, Donald.'

That night when the points for the race were awarded there was a great deal of controversial discussion in the clubhouse. A member claimed that Donald had gripped the rudder of one dinghy in his teeth and actually pulled the boat backwards. However it was Donald's efforts to give one competitor an advantage by pushing him forward that was most hotly debated.

An ancient copy of rules on dinghy racing was consulted. This particular set of rules were drawn up in the heyday of the British Empire when our navy ruled the waves of the world. They were devised to help maintain standards of racing behaviour in such far-flung parts as the River Nile. Thus reference was found about what to do if crocodiles interfered in a race, but absolutely nothing could be found to deal with the participation of a dolphin.

So the following argument ensued.

'I can use the wind to help me win the race can't I?'

'Yes, of course you can,' came the reply.

'The presence of the wind is an act of God isn't it?'

'Well yes, I suppose it is.'

'So you will agree that I can use an act of God to help me win,' said the beneficiary of Donald's help pressing his next point.

'Well I maintain that the presence of the dolphin was also an act of God.'

Before the objector could interrupt he launched forth again.

'So if I can use the wind I can also use the dolphin. That settles it.'

On the basis of this argument the judge's decision was upheld.

The person who thought he had been deprived of points by the antics of the dolphin was later heard holding forth to his cronies in the bar about the serious nature of dinghy racing and how intolerable it was that such interference should be permitted to take place.

If Donald could have heard what ructions he caused I wonder if he would have pondered on the strange character of those men who cannot accept the humorous side of a situation—even when they are playing. If he had done so, I am sure he would have chortled to himself and perhaps blown a raspberry into the air before sinking back into the sea.

When Donald eventually departed from Wales he spent several months in the Percuil River near the picturesque Cornish town of St. Mawes.

He seemed to prefer the area at the mouth of the river and was often seen there by the fishermen early in the morning and late in the day. Donald, boisterous as ever, would swim excitedly round the dinghies when the fishermen rowed out to their fishing boats on the moorings. Most fishermen are prepared to face quite rough weather in order to wrest a living from the seas. However, some of them found Donald's antics too hazardous to risk the journey from the shore to the moorings in their small dinghies for fear of being tipped into the river. They resorted to using much heavier row boats for the trip.

One crew member came close to a ducking when he was making his way out to the moorings in a fast Dory. Donald came out of the water and onto the bows nearly capsizing the plastic boat. This caused the fisherman, who could not swim, lightheartedly to wear a life-jacket on the journeys to and from the big boat.

One person who found the antics of the new arrival very entertaining was Martyn Melhuish. Martyn had a dog called Bunter who would often accompany his master on fishing trips. The fisherman was convinced that his dog could smell Donald's breath at long range because Bunter would bark with excitement if the dolphin was in the river. As Martyn's boat left the shore Donald would charge over, sometimes from hundreds of yards away. When the dolphin came in close to the dinghy, he would stand on his tail, raise his head over the side of the boat and squeak at Bunter. This excited the dog and the dolphin to such an extent that both the fisherman and his pet canine nearly ended up in the water. At times the dolphin became so boisterous that Martyn Melhuish and Bunter were both drenched.

Of all the encounters Martyn had with the mischievous Donald, the one that ranked as the most amazing occurred when the fisherman returned early to base with scallop dredges that needed repair. The crew lowered the dredges, a pair of two metre Frenchmen on a tow bar, into the water to turn them round as there was insufficient room to do so on deck. Donald arrived on the scene and watched fascinated as the crew attempted to manipulate the dredges with a boat hook. The men gesticulated at the dolphin and indicated that they would like his help. After a slight delay Donald put his beak on the tow bars and spun them round as requested.

One of Donald's favourite tricks was to pick up heavy anchors and swim off with the chain draped over his head.

Barry Wills.

After he had done so Donald came alongside squeaking with obvious delight at what he had done. Martyn was not sure if the dolphin really understood what he had been asked. But the fisherman liked to believe he did.

Oyster fishermen in Falmouth, however, did not find Donald so helpful. Some had to abandon fishing one day when Donald decided to take a hand. The technique used by small boats when dredging for oysters is to put out a heavy anchor, move well away from it, and then drop the trawl. Using the anchor as a fixture, the line is hauled in and the trawl is dredged over the sea bed. An obvious problem arises when a dolphin picks up the anchor and swims away—towing the oyster punt behind him.

Another person whose first encounter with Donald was only funny in hindsight was an unsuspecting water skier who suddenly spotted a large triangular fin cutting through the water just ahead of him. Never before had he felt such a need to stay upright, especially when he found that the 'shark' could travel at the same speed and stayed with him despite his most evasive manoeuvres.

However, it was with divers that Donald established his closest contacts. One such person was a friend of mine, Dr. Barry Wills, who lived in Falmouth and was an active member of the local branch of the British Sub-Aqua Club. Barry became very fond of the dolphin. When Donald started to escort the diving boat regularly on short expeditions out of Falmouth, Barry and his fellow divers were delighted and they came to expect the dolphin as part of a regular diving routine. However, not everyone was aware of Donald's newfound alliance with the diving boat *Pisces*. When a novice diver was unexpectedly made the focus of Donald's attention, the results were startling as Barry told me with some relish.

The incident happened on Sunday, 27 November 1977. Barry was supervising a party of nine trainee snorkel and aqualung divers off the rocks of Pendennis Point, Falmouth. Two of the aqualung divers were about 200 yards from the Point, under the steep rocks near Castle Beach when they lost contact with one another. One diver surfaced, but the other broke all the rules and stayed submerged—engrossed in collecting shells from the sandy bottom. It was then that Kevin Martin, a student from the Cambourne School of Mines, felt something gently pushing on his aqualung cylinder. Turning round he was confronted with a huge dark body and an eye about six inches from his mask. Having no previous knowledge of the dolphin his immediate reaction was—shark.

From a vantage point on the rocks Barry and his companions had observed Donald moving from Gylingvase Beach, about a mile away, towards the divers and had seen the dolphin submerge near Kevin's bubbles. A few moments later the group on the rocks burst out laughing when they saw Kevin hit the surface with both hands waving in the air.

The sudden appearance of an open mouth lined with teeth could cause an unsuspecting diver to depart from the scene at an impressive speed.

Horace Dobbs.

The solitary diver then made his way frantically towards the nearby rocks. On reaching them he attempted to claw his way out of the water on his hands and knees with the dolphin seemingly trying to aid his futile efforts by gently prodding him from behind.

It is not hard to imagine the intense relief the novice diver felt when Barry was able to convey to him that the 'shark' was only a playful dolphin. All of the trainee divers promptly joined the dolphin and frolicked with him. To all of them it was a memorable experience.

Donald enjoyed the company of divers, and he quickly learnt which boats had divers onboard. He could certainly tell one vessel from another by their different engine sounds.

The dolphin would often accompany the *Harry Slater* skippered by Keith Roberts, which catered exclusively for divers and had its base in Falmouth. Donald would follow the vessel out of the harbour and escort it to the diving site. During the voyage the divers would excitedly watch

Donald always took a keen interest in any underwater activity involving mechanical gadgets.

Norman Cole.

the dolphin weaving in and out of the bow wave. If, however, an inflatable boat, was being towed behind, Donald showed a distinct preference for the rubber hull and would devote most of his time to escorting the small lightweight craft. Always on such occasions Donald seemed happy, and imbued those on the diving boat with happiness. A sense of excitement and anticipation would build up. Thus, when the divers eventually encountered the dolphin in his environment, they were physically and mentally prepared for his mischievous tricks. Some of the more adventurous ones would hold on to the dolphin's dorsal fin and be towed along by him—always an unforgettable experience. However, Donald was very selective and would not accord this privilege to anyone. If Donald decided he did not want to tow a particular person he would keep well clear, no matter how hard the diver tried to grab him. The secret was not to attempt to dominate the dolphin, but to accept the fact that Donald was the master in the sea.

After I had given a lecture at a diving club near Halifax, one of the audience stood up and told the assembled company, in a very serious manner, that his dive with Donald the dolphin had been the greatest experience of his life. When I requested his name and asked if I could quote his comment he pondered deeply, weighing up the consequences of committing himself so unequivocally.

'Yes you can quote me as saying it was the greatest experience in my life,' he said. Then, after a further pause he added: 'Except for my wedding night.'

This comment drew a burst of raucous laughter from his audience. I could tell from his expression, however, that he had not intended his reply as a joke. And that it was a sincere evaluation of the way in which he related his interaction with Donald relative to the other events in his life.

By the end of 1977 Donald had become a nationally known dolphin and his sometimes outrageous behaviour was a source of amusement and entertainment to those who followed his exploits. This had the advantage for me that I was able to develop a network of contacts who kept me updated on his movements. As the winter closed in, sightings became fewer because of the general decrease in aquatic activities. However, some of the more stalwart divers continued to pursue their recreation in the sea. Here is an account I received from Barry Wills following an exceptional encounter with Donald:

On Saturday 14 January 1978, we found him in perhaps his most playful mood. We were returning from a dive in Falmouth Bay and were joined by Beaky (alias Donald) as we entered Carrick Roads, in the Fal Estuary, to make our way up the river to our mooring at Mylor. Although we were travelling at about six knots, he remained about one foot from our starboard side all the way up to the North Bank buoy, a distance of about one and a half miles. Here four divers entered the water to dive on a submerged wreck, and were immediately joined by Beaky, who rolled onto his back to be stroked, and gave each of them rides, by allowing them to hold onto his dorsal fin. Then they descended 85 feet to dive on the wreck, accompanied by Beaky.

After the dive he again played with them on the surface (for a total time of over an hour) with no signs of becoming bored, as he usually does after a short time.

Three of the divers returned to the boat, leaving him with the *Pisces* skipper, Ken Dunstan. When Ken tried to return to the boat, he prevented him by carrying him off on his back away from the boat.

When the boat moved off to attempt to pick up Ken, he became very excited, and gave us an incredible display of speed and mobility. Moving at enormous speed, his outline just below the surface resembling a huge black arrow, he moved across our bows, leaping out of the water, and then made straight for Ken. Within a couple of feet of Ken,

DONALD'S FAREWELL
On 14 January 1978 Donald played gently with 7 year old Nicola Dunstan. This last recorded contact was photographed by Barry Wills.

still moving at full speed, he suddenly turned through 90 degrees and stopped dead, rather like an ice-skater, throwing a huge wave over Ken. It was as if he was trying to tell us to keep off.

After this awesome display of power, he was at his most gentle when Ken's seven-year-old daughter Nicola entered the water. She soon forgot the cold water (48 F) when Beaky slowly brought his head out of the water and allowed her to stroke it.

Barry was there with his camera to record the scene and he sent me a set of his pictures. I was delighted.

10-year-old Kerry Sergeant of Launceston produced an extravagantly decorated flying dolphin.

On 11 February 1978 I had a 'phone call from Barry informing me of another sighting. Shortly afterwards, one of the worst winter storms on record hit the West Country. Many roads were snowed-up and the winds reached a terrifying force. When they abated and the Falmouth divers made off again, they were sadly disappointed that their regular escort did not join them.

Had Donald moved on again I wondered; and if so where to? I expected news of the dolphin's whereabouts to come through on my countrywide grapevine of diving contacts. But I heard nothing. My efforts to track him down were redoubled following an event which took place in London on 6 June 1978.

One of my contributions to Underwater Conservation Year had been to organise a dolphin competition for the children of Cornwall. The Duke of Cornwall, alias H.R.H. Prince Charles, agreed to judge the finals and the pictures were put on display inside Buckingham Palace.

The pictures were very diverse. They ranged from a small pencil drawing of a cheeky smiling dolphin, through a very sensitive montage of a mother dolphin with her baby, to a large painting of a sea covered with

A humorous dolphin from 7-year-old Lee Oliver whose father was a fisherman in Sennen.

multi-coloured dolphins all performing incredible acrobatics. In addition there were pictures of dolphins leaping in front of rows of round-faced children with hair like twigs and trainers wearing bright red pullovers carrying buckets clearly marked FISH.

When the Prince asked about Donald's present whereabouts I told him that the last sighting had been four months earlier in Falmouth. Even so, he told me he would like to dive with Donald in the sea if he possibly could. As he left the room, he issued instructions for his Equerry to attempt to fit into his crowded diary a rendezvous and dive with Donald the dolphin.

One of the pictures which seemed to depict the humorous nature of a dolphin was drawn by Lee Oliver, the seven-year-old son of a fisherman from Sennen. Lee attended the Sennen County Primary School which produced several other winners.

Shortly after my visit to Buckingham Palace I travelled to Cornwall as I had agreed to show my film of Donald at the winning schools. When I walked into the tiny old-fashioned school at Sennen I was greeted by the headmaster who was taking a class. Later, when I showed my film, which was also shown in Buckingham Palace, I could not help contrasting the crowded Cornish classroom with the spacious splendour of the setting in London. Yet I found both occasions equally rewarding in totally different ways.

After my show in the school I stayed the night at a house nearby with a B & B sign outside. The garage, a wooden and corrugated iron structure, was heeled over at a crazy angle. It looked as if it had been picked up and dropped back down on the ground. When I discussed the subject with my overnight landlady she described the terrifying storm which had indeed literally picked up her garage and moved it from its original position. She said it was the most frightening night she had ever lived through. The wind was so fierce she was afraid it would remove the roof of her house— which was of very solid construction.

The date of the storm coincided exactly with the date of Donald's disappearance from Falmouth. It was 15 February 1978. In cor-respondence with Ian Dunlop, who fished year-round from Helston, I was informed of a 'hell of a gale' which lasted for nearly a week. Even the anchorage in Helford, which is secluded and normally very safe, was filled with breaking swells. My friend Barry Wills also told me about the shrieking winds and how most of the locals, who were accustomed to winter gales, could remember nothing to match it. The storm was accompanied by exceptionally cold weather and parts of Cornwall were cut off for days by drifting snow.

Earlier detective work had shown that Donald had deserted his adopted port of St. Ives in 1976 when gale force winds swept in from the northwest and caused havoc in the harbour. On that occasion he moved round Land's End into the relatively sheltered waters of Carrick Roads, Falmouth. Clearly, the dolphin did not like to stay in places where he could not find quiet water in which to rest. But with a south-easterly gale which raged for days—where would he go? I consulted my map of the area. I then bent my thoughts to the problem of looking for places where Donald might have taken refuge during the storm. The north coast yielded a lee shore but the shoreline did not have the secluded creeks that occur naturally on the south coast of Cornwall.

I decided to visit the most likely places to make enquiries and followed a route along the northern shore. The stone walls which lined the road were tufted with a profusion of foxgloves, honeysuckle and other wild flowers. The rounded hillsides were quilted with a new growth of bright green ferns. In the brilliant June sunshine, the scene was of such tranquillity and beauty it was hard to imagine how fierce the winds could be in this last finger of England. However, the absence of any trees, and the way in which the large roadside shrubs appeared to have had their tops trimmed, testified to the severity and direction of the winter winds which would scythe off any twig or branch that dared to project itself too high towards the heavens.

I visited all of the places in which I thought Donald might have sought shelter from the storm. But nobody had seen the missing dolphin. I telephoned coastguards and many of my contacts who had previously helped me track my nomadic friend, but to no avail. After numerous and intensive enquiries I felt sure that if Donald had still been in Cornish waters someone would have seen him and I would have learned about it.

Had Donald moved much further afield? I launched a national appeal for information and followed-up many clues and dolphin sightings which indicated that he might have journeyed to places as far apart as Kinsale in Ireland and Bayona in Spain. But all of the trails eventually led to the same end-point—no Donald.

About a year after the last sighting of Donald I returned to Falmouth and continued my enquiries about the missing dolphin. Most of the people I talked to told me to go and look in Falmouth Bay. When I did so I understood why Falmouth had been dubbed 'Cornwall's mackerel Klondyke'. The stink of fish meal pervaded the air. It seemed that the horizon no longer consisted of the subtle junction of sea and sky. It was castellated with the silhouettes of fishing boats, foreign factory ships and freezer vessels. I had never before seen such a concentration of large vessels dedicated to the extraction and processing of fish.

The purse-seine techniques used for catching Cornish mackerel were similar to those adopted by the tuna fishermen. With such an enormous number of nets scooping fish from the sea, was it conceivable that Donald had fallen prey to the same perils that had beset so many of the dolphins in the tuna-fished waters of the Pacific? In the scramble for riches would a fisherman who found a dead dolphin amongst the mackerel in his net do any more than curse and toss the body back into the sea? Indeed, what more could he do?

Many of the people I spoke to were very pessimistic about the fate of Donald. The vessels in Falmouth Bay were from many nations including Russia. One lady pointed out to me that as the Russians were prepared to hunt for big whales they would not object to picking up a small one. 'I reckon he's in a can now,' she said dismally. Several other people expressed the same opinion.

I could easily envisage it happening. Donald, with his insatiable curiosity for mechanical things, would have been fascinated by the noise and action of men shooting nets. I remembered that in 1976 I had observed him in St. Ives Bay swimming excitedly round a small trawl net when it was hauled to the surface. Despite the anxiety expressed by the fisherman at the time I felt sure the dolphin would not become trapped because he could scan the entire net with his sonar system and avoid getting into a dangerous situation. This was not so with a very large purse-seine net of the type used off Falmouth, which was very long and deployed to completely encircle large shoals of mackerel. Once inside, there would be no way out for the dolphin when the bottom of the net had been pursed. And Donald who had defied death a dozen times would finally succumb, killed like the proverbial cat, by his own curiosity.

Another view was put to me by a fisherman who liked my fantasy idea that Donald had been sent out from a school of dolphins especially to make contact with man in order that the cetaceans could come to terms with a new force that threatened to destroy them.

'He came, he completed his mission and now he's gone,' he said.

'He's probably swimming around happily in the open sea with a wife and Donald Junior in tow,' he continued.

Being both a romantic and an optimist I prefer to believe that something like that really did happen. I must admit, however, that in my darker hours the other possibility looms like a black cloud across a sunset.

3 SANDY

To my knowledge Donald was the only wild dolphin in the world to associate freely with man for a period of six years (1972–1978). During my own friendship with him I had presented the dolphin with a wide variety of different objects and situations. When I told people about his behaviour a question which was frequently raised was 'How typical is Donald?'

Now scientists do not like conclusions drawn from observations on a single aberrant animal. So I really needed to support my experiments with investigations on other dolphins. The obvious place to conduct such studies was in a dolphinarium with captive dolphins. I was convinced, however, that confinement itself would so change the lifestyle of the dolphins that any observations I might make on their behaviour would certainly be affected by their captive situation and would thus make a comparison of little value. What I needed was another dolphin who was free in the sea yet voluntarily associated with humans.

And I heard of just such a dolphin three days after Christmas Day 1977.

The news came in the form of a 'phone call from Ireland. The lady who telephoned me introduced herself as Sheila Chamberlain. She told me that she and her family had recently returned from San Salvador in the Bahamas where they had a fantastic experience diving with a wild friendly dolphin in the sea. She told me that the local dive leader swam with the dolphin regularly when he escorted parties to a place called Sandy Point. She informed me that the dolphin delighted in the company of divers, but that Sandy as he was called (after Sandy Point) seemed to have a particularly strong affinity with Chris.

I subsequently received some colour prints from Sheila showing the dolphin with her daughter on the surface of the sea. One of the pictures depicted two young swimmers wearing fins, masks and snorkels, floating on the surface of the sea, touching the dolphin with their hands. Only part of the back and the dorsal fin of the dolphin were visible. Although it was obvious that the San Salvador dolphin was considerably smaller than Donald, I could see no other features clearly. Thus its shape, true size, facial features and hence its species remained a mystery.

Some of my questions were answered in a letter from Chris. It arrived when Britain was in the grip of winter, on the very day that the storm which drove Donald out of Falmouth was waging its full fury on Cornwall. Chris enclosed some colour transparencies taken underwater and they were amongst the best undersea pictures of dolphins I had ever seen. The sea had a blue colour which I knew from personal experience is only associated with water of extreme clarity. The divers with the dolphin were wearing no protective clothing, which implied that the water was very warm, and finally the lighting indicated that the sun was shining very brightly on a flat calm surface.

Inevitably my thoughts switched to a comparison between Sandy and Donald, and myself and Chris McLoughlin. I recalled how hard I had to work to develop techniques which would enable me to get pictures of Donald in the relatively murky green waters he frequented. Sometimes, even when wearing a thick wetsuit, I had been driven from the water by the cold. I knew from looking outside at the weather what conditions would be like in the English Channel, where the sea, pounding onto the shore and stirred by the fierce winds, would be full of sediment. This would reduce underwater visibility to a few inches and the light intensity would fall virtually to zero a few feet from the surface. Under such conditions the sea is a most inhospitable environment. Compared to this, pure paradise consists of warm, calm sunny water with that characteristic most prized by all underwater photographers—clarity. And these were the conditions which prevailed five thousand miles away in the Bahamas.

Chris informed me that Sandy was about six feet long and weighed between 150 and 200 pounds. From his overt sexual behaviour he was obviously a male and had been associating with divers from the Riding Rock Inn for about eighteen months. Thus the dolphin would encounter twenty-five to forty different divers a week in addition to the diving guides who regularly escorted their parties to Sandy Point.

From the pictures I was able to see that Sandy enjoyed the presence of divers and his pleasure in their company was expressed in his eyes. Furthermore the shape of his body postures, as he frolicked amongst them, seemed to convey the sense of playfulness which I knew so well with Donald. I could also understand why he had been called a spotted dolphin, because the lower regions were spotted like a poorly marked dalmatian dog. He had the very long beak characteristic of Spinner dolphins which gave his jaw line an exaggerated smile.

In his letter Chris admitted to being 'a dolphin addict of course' and went on to say that 'I've never seen anyone meet him without coming

Sandy enjoyed the company of an expert free diver who could descend into his world wearing only mask, fins and snorkel tube.

Bahamas News Bureau.

away with a very positive feeling inside (vibrations)'. At the end of the letter Chris offered accommodation and free diving if I could find the time and the air fare. If he had dangled a carrot made of solid gold in front of me it could not have further increased my desire to go to the Bahamas to meet Sandy.

I immediately contacted my friend Bruce Lyons, the Managing Director of Twickenham Travel, who organised the travel arrangements for my diving expeditions. Bruce made contact with the Bahamas Tourist Office and I agreed to shoot a 16mm. film of Sandy for them. However, though negotiations went quickly and smoothly, I did have other commitments and it was not until late March that I took off for the Bahamas. A 'phone call to Chris indicated that Sandy was being seen less frequently off Sandy Point and this lengthened the odds of a meeting with the wild dolphin. Nonetheless, when I set off with my seventeen-year-old son Ashley, who was to accompany me as my assistant underwater cameraman, we were both in very good spirits at the prospect of the unknown adventures that were ahead of us.

When we arrived in San Salvador Chris explained that Sandy had not been seen lately, but he was hopeful that the dolphin would join us when we went to Sandy Point. He also pointed out that, as all three diving boats were committed to following their routine dive schedule, he had decided to put Ashley and myself on his boat which would ferry a group of doctors, who were attending a one week course on diving medicine, to the various dive sites around the island.

When we assembled at the jetty the following morning, we discovered just how efficiently the dive and lecture schedules for our group of doctors were organised. Within ten minutes of leaving their lecture the entire group were settled on the boat and we were heading out of the marina towards the open sea. The sun was shining from a sky of unbroken blue on an unruffled sea to match.

Our first dive was to 'The Cathedrals' which consisted of a series of spectacular archways on the edge of the 'drop-off'—the region where the sea suddenly plummets to enormous depths. It was a superb diving site and it provided us with an opportunity to try out our new cine camera and housing before the hoped-for meeting with the dolphin.

The afternoon dive was to a location called Grouper Gully. With cameras in hand, Ashley and I dropped into the clear blue sea to meet the fish after which the site had been named.

That evening in our caravan Ashley and I reviewed the situation. The day of trial dives had revealed faults in our underwater cameras which we managed to correct. Tomorrow was to be the big day—our first visit to Sandy Point where we hoped to encounter Sandy—*the dolphin.*

It was thus with high hopes that we set out the following morning with two powerful engines on the stern of our diving boat pushing it ahead at a fine speed. I was told that if Sandy was in the area he would join the dive boat on its journey to Sandy Point. As every diver onboard had heard of the dolphin and was keen to meet him all eyes were set to scan the ocean for his arrival. Ashley and I did likewise looking first ahead to see if we could detect the joyous rise of the dorsal fin as the dolphin came up to ride the bow wave, and then aft to see if Sandy was enjoying the sensation of having water thrust over his body from the propellers at the stern. But we were disappointed. The dolphin did not appear, and eventually we anchored over the appointed diving site at Sandy Point without the company of Sandy.

Previous diving experience had taught me that the most spectacular underwater scenery is often found around a headland. It is also the place where the biggest fish normally congregate. Although the dolphin had not joined us, I anticipated we would be in for a good dive and I was not disappointed.

The water was exceptionally clear with the underwater visibility in the region of 200 feet. From the surface we could clearly see the bottom immediately beneath us about fifty feet down. We were just on the edge of a reef table which dropped almost vertically to about 140 feet. As we glided down, we could see the underwater vista stretching away from us with unbelievable clarity before it eventually disappeared into a pale blue curtain.

I was hoping that the dolphin would suddenly appear to join in the fun with the divers. So, in addition to enjoying the presence of the multitudinous fish, I took frequent looks into the far distance to see if he was homing in on us. It was on one such scan that I saw a large shape coming from way down the reef. It approached steadily and was making a course in a straight line directly for us. It was a fish called a grouper. When it arrived we were in the company of an Australian doctor who was distributing the last pieces of soggy bread from his food bag. The grouper snapped them up and we started to film. The fish was the largest specimen of a Nassau grouper I had seen.

The grouper stayed with us for the rest of the dive. It was not until we started to head back onto the reef table that the fish suddenly veered off and I watched it return in the direction from which it came. As it disappeared into the azure haze I envisaged him returning to his own special cave deep on the reef.

That evening all of the divers assembled on the patio outside the hotel and I showed the film 'Ride a Wild Dolphin' which I had made with Yorkshire Television about Donald the dolphin. Everyone was most interested to see the wild Bottlenosed dolphin on film and Chris commented how much larger he was than Sandy.

Right up until our last day we were hopeful that Sandy would make a reappearance. But he never did. In fact he was never again seen off San Salvador. What became of him remains a mystery.

Ashley and I consoled ourselves by making a film about a grouper instead of a dolphin. We nicknamed our new star Lord Marmaduke, whom we soon discovered would perform extraordinary antics, such as having a tug-of-war, in his efforts to secure food. The fish's behaviour contrasted with that of Donald the dolphin who would never accept any food—no matter what tasty morsels we offered him.

The Nassau grouper we nicknamed Lord Marmaduke had a tug-of-war with Ashley when offered some sausages threaded on a string.

Horace Dobbs.

Although I failed to make personal contact with Sandy I was keen to pursue my investigation of the connection between humans and dolphins. I therefore set out to collect what information I could on the effect Sandy had on the people he met in the sea. One person who was most helpful in this respect was a lady who set-up a permanent diving facility called Pat's Place on San Salvador shortly after we left.

Pat wrote to me from her new home and here is her own account of her contact with Sandy, which she prefaced as 'a moving spiritual experience that is difficult to narrate objectively'.

We first met Sandy in December of 1976 when he would appear, leading the boat at Sandy Point. When I went over the side, camera in hand, he would disappear. When the boat began moving again, he would reappear.

It was in Feb/March 1977 that Sandy began to approach snorkellers and divers and every time I saw him from there on his progression in contact with humans was remarkable. I fully expected to see him driving the boat!

In July of '77 I took Chris Adair to San Sal to meet and photograph Sandy. Sandy adored Chris because he could free dive to 110 feet. He preferred skin divers—perhaps he knew that they weren't cheating with tanks! One day Chris Adair was free diving with Sandy and the dolphin took him deeper than usual. He pointed with his beak to the reef directly below him—there was the cross that Chris had been wearing around his neck—the chain had broken and we surmised that Sandy had attempted to catch the cross in the water as it fell, because it was indented with several of his teeth marks.

While Chris was there in July 1977, so was Paul Tzimoulis. He asked us to keep Sandy around after our photography so that his photo class could take some pictures. When they arrived (in many clouds of sand) Sandy greeted them all, but suddenly disappeared.

Chris McLaughlin and Chris Adair went to find him, and discovered him trying to support a woman in Paul's class who was in trouble on the surface. She had to be towed in by Chris McLoughlin.

On one occasion in Sept of '77 I went into the water to see Sandy. He did his usual pulling of hair, rubbing his body up against mine (a very horny male!) and giving me a ride. Before long I realised that he had very cleverly drawn me close to a mile from the boat. When I surfaced, the boat was a tiny speck on the horizon. It was a slong swim back! With no help from my beloved friend who would always tow me away from the boat—never towards it.

Very often, after someone left the water, Sandy would "pout" and go to no-one for a while.

The most remarkable characteristic of Sandy in my mind, was his ability to understand and "sense" each person's water ability and personality. He never played rough with those who couldn't handle it. He definitely preferred certain people over others. One would know beforehand who he would prefer if one was aware of their personality traits. Warm, loving people enjoyed Sandy the most. The feeling was always mutual. The other outstanding characteristic was his fantastic sense of humour. Hair pulling, mask grabbing, a gentle crack on the head with his beak. Deliberately making it difficult to take pictures.

When I read Pat's letter for the first time I felt that if she substituted the name Donald for Sandy she could have been referring to my Bottlenose friend instead of her spotted companion. For instance Donald preferred to play with Ashley and I when we were not wearing our aqualungs and would free dive with him. There was just one small area where the two dolphins appeared to differ. Donald would tow us back to the boat as well as away from it. There were certainly occasions when Donald did not want us to leave the water. The dolphin would grab our fins between his teeth and pull us back into the water when we attempted to climb back into the boat.

However, my most cherished memory of Donald was his sense of humour. I was delighted to hear that Sandy had a similar disposition. Perhaps it is this characteristic above all others which differentiates man's relationship with the dolphin from that of all other animals. Many domestic and wild animals have a sense of fun, which is often infectious. Thus when dogs or kittens are playing with humans both sides can enjoy the game and the fun derived from it. But a sense of humour is normally regarded as an exclusively human trait.

Lord Marmaduke, the Nassau grouper, the underwater territorial ruler of Sandy Point had been a source of fun and amusement to the divers, but it was a very one-sided relationship in this respect. There was no question that the fish ever derived any sensations akin to fun or amusement from our presence. His sole reward was to satisfy a basic need to fill his belly. Any curiosity he possessed was directed towards this end. His small primitive brain had not developed the mysterious sense that we call humour—which is extremely difficult to define— and almost impossible

The dolphin connection. Sandy would allow only certain people to touch him.

Chris McLoughlin.

to measure. It is perhaps pertinent that we refer to humour as a sense—yet it is not included in our five basic senses—sight, sound, touch, smell and taste.

Playing involves physical and sometimes mental exercise, which can involve all five basic senses yet is often devoid of humour. Humour is an experience which is probably perceived via the frontal lobe of the cerebral cortex of the brain. As man and dolphin are both equipped with comparable frontal lobes it is conceivable that the positive intellectual interplay which we call humour, can take place between the two species.

This leads to the interesting speculation that the need for intellectual interplay is one of the prime motivating forces which leads to solitary wild dolphins seeking and maintaining human contact. Thus if dolphins enjoy the pleasure associated with a developed sense of humour when they are in a social group of their own kind, what happens when they become isolated? Regardless of the reason for their isolation, they will certainly not find the mental satisfaction they are seeking with their fellow occupants of the marine environment—the fish. So was it Sandy's innate sense of humour that caused him to seek out Pat Selby? She also had sensitivity, which is the other, perhaps even more important pre-requisite for the build-up of a human–dolphin relationship.

The human–dolphin connection is made with a wild dolphin off San Salvador in the Bahamas.

Chris McLoughlin.

Friendly wild Bottlenosed dolphin in the Red Sea. He led us a merry dance.

Horace Dobbs.

We tried to see how Donald would react to being touched by different textures, such as the bristles on a brush, but he was always more interested in playing games.

Horace Dobbs.

We found Donald cruising amongst the boats in shallow water in Coverack.

We hoped to find the dolphin near a small wreck off Coral Island.

Top   *Dorothy Skinner.*

Bottom   *Horace Dobbs.*

Donald enjoyed the company of swimmers as well as divers in Coverack — sometimes with startling consequences.

For committing the crime of eating fish dolphins are executed by Japanese fishermen off the island of Iki.

Top   *Horace Dobbs.*

Bottom   *Dexter Cate.*

Stranded dolphin corpses – Dexter Cate looks sadly on.

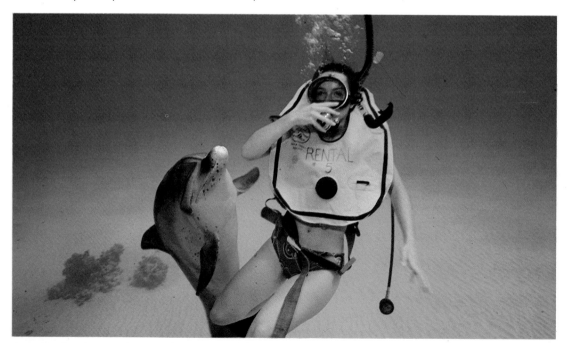

A novice diver is not quite sure what to make of Sandy's friendly advances.

Top   *Suzie Cate.*

Bottom   *Chris McLoughlin.*

When there was no human activity Donald would amuse himself playing with a boat and a mooring buoy.

When we at last made contact with the wild dolphin in the Red Sea I felt I had known him for a long time.

Top   *Horace Dobbs.*

Bottom   *Chris Goosen.*

Donald poses for a picture over a forest of kelp.

A snorkel diver offers Horace a piece of seaweed to play with off Napier in New Zealand.

Top   *Horace Dobbs.*

Bottom   *Quentin Bennett.*

4   HORACE IN NEW ZEALAND

Less than one year after my visit with Ashley to the Bahamas to find the elusive Sandy I heard of another solitary dolphin seeking the company of man. The news came from a part of the world that was even further away from England—New Zealand.

In December 1978 the following headline appeared in the *New Zealand Herald*: HORACE THE DOLPHIN STEALS THE SHOW. It was a report from Napier and it announced that spectacular shows were being put on, close inshore, by a free ranging wild Bottlenosed dolphin. The dolphin had chosen to entertain the public, free of charge, 100 yards off Westshore beach just outside the Napier dolphinarium where visitors paid to see captive dolphins leaping.

> night after night Horace has been turning on his act of aerial flips and great leaps out of the water as he frolics with divers and boats that have become his playmates.

Horace delighted in the company of swimmers and occasionally allowed them to touch him. He did not permit more than glancing contact and, when a diver tried to grab his dorsal fin, the dolphin slapped the surface of the water with his tail in an obvious sign of displeasure. He would go racing across to people who tapped the sides of their boats and responded with extra leaps when onlookers cheered excitedly. A television crew turned up to film Horace's antics and many of the public who saw the footage were surprised to learn that dolphins do not need trainers to make them perform. 'It all comes naturally,' was the newspaper comment.

Horace the dolphin seemed to have a mischievous sense of humour. He discovered that nudging the rudder of a sailing dinghy underway produced a good response that was highly amusing to any onlookers although the joke was not always shared by those onboard. His sense of humour found even greater expression when the dolphin discovered that he could produce havoc by pushing up the centre boards of small dinghies under sail. The more the crews protested the more Horace appeared to enjoy the mischief. One person who was particularly annoyed by the dolphin's practical jokes was a local Anglican Bishop. He was sailing his Sunburst dinghy, when Horace pushed the centreboard up with such force that he split it. Nonetheless, most of those upon whom Horace focused his attention took the wild dolphin's tricks in good part and enjoyed the experience of having the company of such an unusual and playful companion.

One of the people who was more than delighted at the new arrival close to his home in Taradale was Frank Robson, a man who had devoted much of his later life to the study of dolphins and their close relatives the

Horace

In recent months Horace the Bottlenose dolphin has chosen to make the coastal waters off Napier's Westshore home. He was first seen to the north off Whirinaki beach during September. Since then he has moved towards the city and up to people.

A local expert estimates him to be a four to five year old bull, fully mature but at three metres and 200 kilograms not quite fully grown.

For Horace and the people of Napier the relationship seems poised to add to the tales that go to make myths and legends — stories of cheerful friendships between sailors and dolphins at sea, of dolphins coming ashore to play with children and carrying them on their backs and of dolphins rescuing men at sea and bringing them to shore.

But like all tales they can have a dark side.

In 1955 the people of Opononi and a dolphin befriended one another in Hokianga Harbour. Like Horace Opo, as that dolphin came to be named, was an isolate either lost or outcast from the family group.

By Christmas 1955, at the height of the holiday season, Opo could be relied on to appear almost every day. The local people were quick to form a protection committee and notices were erected asking for careful behaviour. The idyllic summer continued.

But on 9 March Opo was found dead cut to shreds and jammed in a crevice on the rim of a rock pool. It was commonly believed though never openly stated, that self interest and commercial considerations had led someone to kill the dolphin with a gelignite blast.

Of course we hope that the tragedy of Opononi will not be repeated at Westshore.

It is for this and other reasons that this brochure has been published so as to provide information on dolphins particularly the Bottlenose in the belief that informed and aware people are caring people.

Some of the citizens of Napier were concerned that their new friendly dolphin – named Horace after the author – would suffer the same fate as Opo. As a result pamphlets describing how to treat the friendly wild dolphin were distributed.

large whales. Before Horace's arrival, Frank and I had become long-distance friends with the letters we exchanged half-way round the world. We quickly established that we had common attitudes to dolphins. Frank was fascinated by the marine mammals that he regularly encountered when to took his fishing boat to sea. He had a passion to learn about them and help what he considered to be to most beautiful creatures on earth—the dolphins and whales.

Boy on a dolphin. Opo gives a youngster a ride.
New Zealand Newspapers Ltd.

From his letters and other reports I had read, I deduced that Frank was an outspoken man who was not slow to aim criticism at those in authority when he felt that either through ignorance or greed they were causing harm or death to his beloved dolphins. When Horace made his first appearance off Napier, Frank was concerned for the well-being of the newly arrived dolphin. Frank therefore set about establishing a special personal relationship with the marine mammal. Knowing of my own friendship with Donald, it was Frank who gave the dolphin the name of Horace. When I heard I could not have been more flattered. I know of no-one else who has had the honour of having a dolphin named after him.

At first Horace tended to stay well offshore and each day Frank went out to find the dolphin in order to build-up their relationship. Frank discovered that the dolphin sometimes carried objects around in his mouth. So the fisherman kept in his boat a frond of kelp that he would give to the dolphin to play with. Soon the dolphin trusted his human friend and would follow Frank's boat. It was not long before Frank was able to entice the dolphin into shallow water where Horace could enjoy the company of holidaymakers who swam out from the beach. Horace became a local celebrity. When the media publicised the dolphin's amusing antics, Frank Robson became very concerned for the safety of Horace and, with the support of the Commission for the Future and the Commission for the Environment, a leaflet was produced and distributed free in Napier. It was entitled simply HORACE. It explained the dolphin's arrival and that Horace was about three metres long and had an estimated weight of 200 kg.

In addition to giving general facts and figures on dolphins the pamphlet contained details of a cautionary tale. It concerned Opo the dolphin whose antics with children delighted the world when they saw the pictures and read the story in newspapers and magazines. But as Frank pointed out in his pamphlet, there was also a dark side to this romantic association between man and dolphin. This is how it was described in the pamphlet:

> In 1955, at the height of the holiday season, Opo could be relied on to appear almost every day. The local people were quick to form a protection committee and notices were erected asking for careful behaviour. The idyllic summer continued.
>
> But on 9 March Opo was found dead cut to shreds and jammed in a crevice on the rim of a rock pool. It was commonly believed, though never openly stated, that self interest and commercial considerations had led someone to kill the dolphin with a gelignite blast.
>
> Of course we hope that the tragedy of Opononi will not be repeated at Westshore.
>
> It is for this and other reasons that this brochure has been published so as to provide information on dolphin particularly the Bottlenose in the belief that informed and aware people are caring people.

In his pamphlet Frank also pointed out that if the citizens of Napier wished to retain their new aquatic entertainer they too should be sensitive to the dolphin's moods and requirements.

Although such statements as: 'Treat Horace as you would your best

Opo surrounded by bathers at Opononi during the idyllic summer of 1955. A few months later the dolphin was blown to pieces, probably deliberately, with a gelignite blast.

New Zealand Newspapers Ltd.

friend', 'Don't force yourself upon him' and 'Be gentle at all times' were read with some jocularity in the Dobbs' household, we all admired the pamphlet. We were also impressed with the initiative Frank and his colleagues had shown in their efforts to save the wild dolphin from accidents that could arise through ignorance.

For one of Napier's best known divers—Quentin Bennett—a single headline in Frank's pamphlet was especially appropriate. It read as follows: 'Look after Horace and you will be part of a rare experience'. Quentin's first contact was made when the dolphin took the diver's fins in his mouth and tugged them. Later the two of them started to play games with one another that at times became very boisterous. In a letter to me Quentin explained how on one occasion he saw stars when in the middle of a jack-knife dive he collided head-on with the dolphin. Despite this painful incident Quentin continued to play with Horace and was rewarded by a number of magnificent rides with the diver clinging to the dolphin's dorsal fin. Quentin did not use an aqualung during these activities. He wore a wetsuit, plus fins, mask and snorkel. Thus, like a dolphin, he could stay submerged only for as long as he could hold his breath. An extra tinge of excitement was added to these thrilling rides because Horace usually took Quentin down to the sea bed. As the underwater visibility was only a few feet, the diver rushed forward in the gloom not knowing where his supercharged mount was taking him.

Some other divers who were treated in a similar fashion found the experience very unnerving and declined further rides. Indeed Horace had his favourite human playmates. Any would-be jockeys whom the dolphin did not like, usually because they were too rough with him, were given such a hefty thump with his tail that they left the water and declined to dive with the dolphin again.

To Quentin, who was fit and willing to engage in an underwater rough and tumble, the highlight of his dolphin experiences came when Horace picked him up and carried the exhilarated diver back to his boat much to the amazement of his goggle-eyed children onboard.

Horace the dolphin also befriended another human who was a complete contrast to the fit aquatic Quentin Bennett. She was a lady who was extremely nervous of the water and could in no way be described as a diver. Yet such was the affinity she felt for the dolphin that she overcame all her fears and established a relationship with the dolphin in the water. Her name was Rosamond Rowe, whom I came to know as Ros.

Rosamond's interest in the dolphin started when her husband, Allan, swam with Horace and the two of them developed a mutual trust. Allan would swim out into deep water and play hide-and-seek with the dolphin in the seaweed. When that game was over the two mammals would have a tug-of-war contest using a piece of kelp to take the strain of their opposed forces. If one of the contestants let go the other would dash off with the 'rope'. Horace tried all sorts of tricks and loved the fun. Sometimes when Allan appeared on the shore and called, the dolphin would dash off to return with a piece of seaweed in anticipation of the games to follow.

One day, shortly after one of Allan's early swims with Horace, the dolphin swam in close to the beach where the Rowe family were enjoying a picnic with an elderly friend, Miss Bingham. When they saw Allan swimming with the dolphin, the two ladies felt an overwhelming desire to join in the fun. But neither of them had their swimming costumes. So with a hesitant glance at the busy highway forty yards away, they stripped to their underwear and rushed into the sea. Horace's trust had not developed to a stage where he would venture into very shallow water and the Napier housewife and her elderly friend had to be content with watching Horace playing in water which was out of their depth.

It was not until the dolphin came into the harbour that Ros established her first real contact with Horace. She spoke to the dolphin and sensed that he was responding to her verbal overtures.

Encouraged by Horace's friendliness, the Rowe family purchased a small rowing boat for the express purpose of enabling them to watch the dolphin more closely. During the Easter holiday of 1979 the Rowes were able to get alongside the dolphin and Horace allowed Ros to caress him all over as she talked gently to him.

Such were the effects of this close contact that Ros purchased a wetsuit. Wetsuits are made of sponge neoprene and, in addition to keeping the wearer warm, they make him/her buoyant. A wetsuit can therefore be regarded as a thermal lifejacket. With just a few pounds of lead on a weightbelt Ros felt comfortable in the water and could bob around quite happily and safely. Thus she was able to join Horace in his own element. The dolphin seemed to appreciate this bold step by the housewife who in her turn was thrilled to share an interspecies friendship.

The first time Ros was given a ride by Horace happened on a day of special significance because it was the one on which she learned that a horse she had owned several years earlier, and which had been a beloved companion to her, had died. Ros felt very flat when she heard the news and agreed to join the family when they suggested a rowing boat trip to find the dolphin. When Horace was located he was in one of his most trusting and playful moods. Ros decided to do something she had been wanting to do for ages but felt silly about. She sat quietly in the boat and sang to him. Horace was fascinated and lay quietly on the surface with the pinhole of his ear exposed. Ros then let herself into the water and was immediately approached by Horace who swam underneath her and took her on his back. It was not until he surfaced that she realised she was sitting between his blowhole and his dorsal fin.

Perhaps even more remarkable than the friendship between the dolphin and Ros, was the relationship Horace developed with the Rowe's friend— the seventy-year-old Miss Bingham. For the elderly lady also acquired a wetsuit and enjoyed aquatic games with Horace. As the Rowe's young children also participated in the activities it could be said that Horace's relationships bridged three generations of humans.

Every one of Horace's human friends hoped he would stay in Hawke Bay for a long time but they all knew his visit could come to a sudden end. Indeed, I too hoped that Horace would stay in Napier long enough for me

Mrs Rosamond Rowe, left, and Miss Margaret Bingham with Horace in the Inner Harbour, Napier.

Allan Rowe.

to organise a visit to New Zealand to meet my namesake face to face.

But it was not to be.

For some time divers had been laying charges in the harbour. Frank Robson and others, concerned for the dolphin's safety, asked for advance warning before charges were detonated underwater in order that they could entice the dolphin away. However, they were not always notified and Horace's many friends were worried that the dolphin would either be killed or maimed by the shock waves if he was close to a charge when it went off.

The Rowes and Miss Bingham had their last swim with Horace on Saturday, 26 May 1979. The humans noted that their dolphin companion did not behave normally and appeared to be wary of physical contact. At dusk on 7 June, after an absence of two weeks, Miss Bingham saw Horace feeding offshore. Six hours later, 600 metres away another explosion took place in the harbour.

Whether or not the dolphin was killed by the explosion, which seems unlikely as no body was recovered, or simply moved on, nobody knows. It was suggested in the New Zealand press that Horace may have migrated to warmer waters.

Many of the people of Napier sadly missed the dolphin, whom they had come to regard as their own special friend. Those who made extra special efforts to help and befriend the dolphin will find that the memories of the pleasures they shared will become more valuable as the years pass. Margaret Bingham, ever hopeful that Horace would return, expressed her feelings in a poem entitled *Seeking Horace*

Perhaps he'll come today—
perhaps I'll see the fin
cleaving towards me
or the swirl
where the honing body has
just been;
feel the skin so smooth
and underneath
the bone of muscle.
Courteously
he'll come, leaving
the darting fish to
say holloa;
nudge me with his beak
or take my foot
into his mouth saying
I love you—
then like the wind
under the water
go
to his own encounters.

Margaret Bingham

5 INTERNATIONAL DOLPHIN WATCH

A feature that was common to Donald, Sandy and Horace was that nobody knew where they came from, or where they went when they disappeared. This reflects a much broader general lack of knowledge of dolphins—a point which was brought to focus by Prince Charles, during my visit to Buckingham Palace.

As we passed from one panel to another, discussing the merits of the different entries in the dolphin competition, Prince Charles interspersed his comments with general enquiries on dolphins; such question as:

'How many are there around the British Isles?'

'Where do they come from?'

'Where do they go to?'

'Where do they give birth to their young?'

'How long do they live in the wild?'

To all of the questions I had to reply 'I don't know.'

'I thought you were an expert,' he quipped.

'That's right, I am,' I replied. 'But the truth of the matter is that nobody knows.'

It could be argued that the fact that we know next to nothing about the life of wild dolphins in the sea is probably beneficial to the dolphins. For when the paths of man and dolphins cross more often than not it spells disaster to the dolphins. Indeed man is their only real enemy. And in recent years man has decimated dolphin populations both directly and indirectly, deliberately and accidentally.

One of the dilemmas was poignantly expressed in an essay from a nine-year-old boy, Antony Chapman, who submitted his entry to my dolphin competition from Saltash Junior School. Here it is:

Dolphins

I'm a hunted dolphin. As I look around me I see the shadows of motorboats. I look up, I see yellow faces and slanted eyes. Suddenly I hear a squeal! One of the school is already dead. The other dolphins go to help while I investigate. I rise to the surface of the water but see nothing. Then suddenly out of nowhere a speedboat comes charging at me. It's trying to kill as it did the other dolphin. I must go and warn the others. Meanwhile up above the Japanese are circling in their boat. Then I see a flush of bubbles. A man tries to kill me with a harpoon. I swim into deep water where he can't get me. Then I come out. It looks all clear to me I say but it isn't. For behind some seaweed hides the man. He catches me with his harpoon. It looks like the end of my life.

Antony Chapman's essay was undoubtedly inspired by an event which took place in Japan on 23 February 1978. The barbaric treatment of dolphins shocked and disgusted millions of people throughout the world. Some of those affected, the older people, were still haunted by memories of atrocities carried out by the Japanese on prisoners during the Second World War. However, many of those most affected were very young people like Antony Chapman with relatively little knowledge of the history and culture of those responsible for a deliberate attempt to eradicate dolphins from their seas.

It happened when a fisherman discovered a dolphin following a shoal of yellowtail fish in the waters of Tsushima Strait. He harpooned the mammal and raised the alarm. When a group of dolphins gathered round to assist their stricken companion more than 100 fishing boats closed in on the dolphins and started to drive them towards Iki Esland off Northern Kyushu.

To the Japanese fishermen the dolphins were an enemy that had to be destroyed. The drive and subsequent dolphin slaughter were conducted like a military operation. It started at about 3 p.m. on Thursday, 24 February. Deploying their boats like platoons of soldiers, the Japanese rounded-up the dolphins in the area and forced them into a small bay. Isolating boats were then rushed to the scene and the mouth of the bay was sealed with nets. There the captured dolphins were imprisoned until 8.30 a.m. the following day. By this time about one thousand fishermen were on hand to help with the massacre.

The following morning I opened *The Daily Telegraph* at my breakfast table and read about the happenings on the previous day under the headline JAPANESE CLUB 1,000 DOLPHINS TO DEATH. In the lengthy article which had been sent from a correspondent in Tokyo, I learned how the dolphins were driven ashore two or three at a time, dragged up the beach and left for later killing at the hands of the club-wielding fishermen.

The fishermen explained to the journalist that 'they considered dolphins to be "gangsters of the sea" because they eat cuttlefish and yellowtail fish.'

His article continued as follows:

As the angry fishermen proceeded from dolphin to dolphin with their clubs, butting the crying mammals on their heads, they were absolutely untouched by the tears which streamed from the eyes of the dolphins on shore.

Later, the heads were chopped off, the bodies gutted and the dolphin carcasses tied to concrete blocks and dumped back into the sea.

Those who were upset by the articles in the newspapers, which were accompanied by black and white photographs, had their sensitivities even more strongly disturbed in the evening when the same news item was shown on television. The incident was reported on film and viewers with colour sets saw the water red with blood from the bleeding dolphins. It was a harrowing sight.

Not unexpectedly the Iki massacre, as it became known, produced a wave of public indignation and reaction against both the fishermen of Iki and the Japanese in general. The Japanese embassy was bombarded with protests. I was invited to appear on the BBC programme *Tonight* and, in an interview with Dennis Tuohy, I showed a clip of my film of Donald. As the newsfilm illustrating the slaughter of the dolphins at Iki was also included in the item, the contrast between the two situations—man in harmony with dolphins and man in conflict with dolphins—could not have been more grotesque.

It was not difficult to trace the events on the other side of the world which led to government authorities putting a bounty on the head of every dolphin. Iki indirectly followed the developments which took place after the Second World War when Japan became one of the world's major producers of consumer goods. It was a road to financial glory for which the price was degradation of the staffs of life—air and water. The Tokyo air became heavy with lead from petrol fumes and the seas around were used as a dumping ground for mercury and other chemical wastes. By the early 1960s widespread pollution had wiped out many of Japan's coastal fishing grounds. Thus pressure was put on the Iki fishermen to produce even more fish from their relatively uncontaminated waters which were already giving up their maximum sustainable yield of yellowtail fish.

In hindsight the result was as predictable as it was inevitable. The fish became scarcer and the frustration of those who for generations had been solely dependent upon fishing for their livelihoods turned on the dolphins.

Despite the enormous volume of protests which their action provoked in 1978, the fishermen were determined to continue their war on the dolphins, and further bloody slaughters took place in 1979 and 1980.

DON'T MURDER DOLPHINS

Many people were shocked when they heard of the massacre of the dolphins by the Japanese. Jenny Crates started her own campaign and quickly won a lot of support using a display sticker with a very direct message.

One of the witnesses to the 1980 dolphin massacre was John Edwards, a reporter from *The Daily Mail*. Knowing that John Edwards had also frolicked in the sea with Donald I found his graphic description of the scenes even more disturbing.

Here is how John Edwards described what for him was a nightmare.

The huge dawn sun of Japan rose into the clear sky and glazed the sea. There were so many fishing boats heading for the dolphins it looked like an invasion force.

When they rendezvoused ten miles out there were 900 boats in the area three miles wide slipping quietly behind a herd of dolphins which was so big the sea boiled from horizon to horizon. Four men were in each boat.

Boats at the end of the arc pulled towards the middle. Now the fleet was like the shape of the horns of a bull sweeping a seaful of leaping dolphins in front of them.

The fishermen screamed at them. They dipped iron pipes into the water and banged them with hammers. The noise exploded under water sending shockwaves like gunfire to frighten the great creatures into a terrifying fight for their lives.

The trap closed around them. The boats steered them into the narrow creek of Thatsuno island. The sea was a wild sight of thrashing dolphins.

Babies were pushed to the surface by their mothers to stop them being crushed.

Then a net was dropped from one side of the creek to the other. It penned over a thousand dolphins between the sea and the beach.

"It was a sight I could not have imagined," recalled fisherman Yamanda. And the curtain rose on the real horror of the day.

Suddenly, the fishermen went chest deep into the water. They hacked the dolphins with axes and cleavers and stabbed them with poles which had iron spikes nailed to the end.

The sea went red. It was so thick with entrails and dolphin foetuses it didn't look like water any more.

The dolphins rose painfully trying to escape. They snorted for air and corkscrewed at the net that was holding them and tried to leap for safety with their stomachs trailing and tail fins cut off.

The bloody smears of their victory covered the bodies of the fishermen. Dolphins were dragged onto the beach and left to pant to death in the sun. Baby dolphins were thrown onto the rocks.

The awful noise of killing and screaming and the stench lay in the creek like a war in hell.

The urge for revenge grew in the fishermen. They went on hacking and stabbing and the rising tide took the stain of the slaughter high on to the rocks.

The last dolphins were dragged to a lung-bursting death on the beach, or had their insides flushed out with a knife.

At the time John Edwards was compiling his report for London a daring attempt was made to save the lives of at least some of the dolphins. The man in the front line of the commando-style rescue operation was a thirty-six-year-old American marine scientist and former teacher, Dexter Cate.

Cate carried a small inflatable plastic kayak together with collapsible paddles hidden in his back-pack when he landed on the island of Iki, 1,200 miles south-west of Tokyo, where the dolphins were corralled and awaiting execution.

Gasping dolphins await execution by Japanese fishermen.

Suzie Cate, Greenpeace.

Cate, a member of the Greenpeace Foundation, waited until the fishermen stopped work for the day before putting on his wet-suit. Under the cover of darkness he paddled his flimsy craft a mile through high surf to the mouth of Tatsuno-shima Bay. There he slipped overboard into the bitterly cold water and managed to untie and cut some of the ropes of the nets that imprisoned the dolphins.

Even when the way to freedom was opened, many of the prisoners were reluctant to leave their injured companions. Dexter Cate had to swim amongst the confused dolphins urging them to escape, but many refused to run for freedom.

Hours later, the exhausted Cate could not make it back to base. High winds and large waves forced him ashore. The next morning, when the fishermen returned to continue the slaughter, they discovered Cate, cold and fatigued, and took him to their village. There were reports of a menacing crowd gathering as the fishermen interrogated Cate in the fishing co-operative's hall. He was later arrested by the police who further interrogated him.

Dexter Cate was subsequently charged with 'forceful obstruction of the fishermen's business.' He was refused bail and when he went on hunger strike was force fed. A month later his trial started and on 30 May he was given a six month sentence suspended for three years. After the verdict he was handed over to the immigration authorities who deported him on the grounds that his visa had expired. After more than three months in a Japanese jail Dexter Cate returned home to Hawaii.

The imprisonment of Dexter Cate without bail incensed many conservation groups throughout the world. In Britain Jenny Crates, founder member of Dolphin Defence organised a petition and gathered thousands of signatures. She also led a delegation of Members of Parliament and show business stars to lodge a protest at the Japanese Embassy in London. Many of the protesters, who could do nothing directly to help the dolphins, admired Dexter Cate as a man who was prepared to take effective action and pay the price.

The Japanese Foreign Ministry in London revealed that the number of dolphins caught in 1978 was 1,327 and this rose to 1,621 in 1979 with a further increase to 1,818 in 1980. Information concerning the subsidies paid to fishermen was also released. It amounted to Y20,000 (£42) for every dolphin killed. According to the Japanese Minister of Information this was intended to offset the loss of the fishermen's earnings caused by the decline of the yellowtail catches. In practice the subsidy acted as a formidable financial incentive to kill more dolphins. When the organisation Friends of the Earth looked into the level of payment it was discovered that on average the subsidy from six dead dolphins represented one person's entire income from fishing for one year.

When this information was coupled with the fact that the government contributed $70,000 towards a machine for use by the Matsumoto Fisheries Co-operative to grind dolphins into pig feed and fertiliser, the seriousness of the Japanese Dolphin Eradication Programme could not be denied. GENOCIDE AGAINST DOLPHINS was how one American organisation captioned a picture of the newly installed machine which was named 'Auschwitz'.

Life in the sea is a very complicated matrix of interdependent species. Nature has shown time and time again, on the land and in the sea, that the selective removal of a single species to solve a short-term problem often creates long-term problems of far greater magnitude.

In the old fishing community at Iki there was a legendary taboo against killing dolphins. The village elders maintained that to break the taboo was to court maritime disaster. Old rites and superstitions often have a hidden logic. It is possible that, when the present day fishermen of Iki broke the taboo, changes which would bring personal disaster to many of them were already written in the stars.

The Japanese regarded the dolphins as their enemies. To other fishermen, however, the dolphins are allies because they help them locate much prized tuna fish.

In the eastern Pacific Ocean large shoals of tuna are often accompanied by dolphins. Why this partnership was formed is still a mystery. It has been suggested that they were both following the same food resource. But this seems too facile an explanation. I suspect that careful and detailed observations will eventually reveal a much more complex interplay between the dolphins—which are aquatic mammals, and the tuna— which are true fish. However, if man continues the present volume of tuna fishing with the techniques now in use, a possibly mutually beneficial association of sea creatures could be destroyed in a decade.

This new dilemma for the dolphins can be traced back to 1927 when the albacore tuna did not appear as usual off the coast of California. The small US fleet which set out to intercept the migrating fish sailed far south in search of the vanished stocks. In the deep blue expanse of the eastern tropical Pacific, which was untouched by fishing, the fishermen discovered the huge yellowfin tuna in almost undreamed-of abundance. It must have been an exciting moment when the dolphins were spotted. For dolphins (usually referred to as porpoises in the USA) on the water, and flocks of sea birds in the air, marked for unseen tuna below.

When the cry 'Porpoises' rang out the crew would burst into a frenzy of activity as the vessel headed straight for the dolphins. With the dolphins around the ship, the crew would fish either with long lines, or with very strong fishing rods (called poles in the USA). In the latter method, bait would be scattered in the water and, once the tuna were in a feeding frenzy, they would take the bare barbless hooks hung from poles wielded by the crew who would then swing the heavy fish aboard. And whilst they stayed with the dolphins the crew would work strenuously to haul one fighting fish after another onto the deck. It was extremely exhausting work, but the crews were well paid and financial rewards for the owners of successful tuna boats were considerable. This method of fishing had no known harmful effects on the dolphins marking the tuna.

In the 1930s, when the United Stated was in the throes of the Great Depression, the tuna fishermen enjoyed a bonanza. Many a tuna man must have blessed the dolphins for the providential role they played in the provision of uncommon prosperity. For nearly three decades the American tuna fishermen dominated tuna fishing in the Eastern Pacific. They had a virtual monopoly for their product in a huge home market. And the rest of the world was hungry for cans of tuna which competed favourably with canned salmon.

The rivals to the Americans were the Japanese who started to build their own armada of tuna clippers after the Second World War. By the mid 1950s economic storm clouds started to form over the American industry as the Japanese-caught tuna flooded onto the market and depressed the price. But the storm did not break. For the Americans were able to take advantage of years of experiment, coupled with post-war technological inventions such as nylon nets and power blocks which could haul huge loads. Using their new knowledge and equipment, the Americans developed a novel technique for catching tuna based on the purse seine net. This method was much less labour intensive than the pole and long line fishing techniques. It gave the Americans an economic edge over their competitors. By 1960, although a considerable number of bait boats remained, the majority of the ever-expanding US Fleet was equipped with purse seine nets, which could bring in as much as 100 tons of tuna in a single shoot.

Once a school of dolphins was located they were 'rounded-up' cowboy style using four or five speedboats instead of horses. The dolphins were herded to a position alongside the parent boat and allowed to 'settle down' with the tuna circling restlessly below. The school of dolphins and

Huge nets are used to capture tuna; sadly many dolphins are also caught and die.

Horace Dobbs.

their accompanying tuna were then encircled with a huge net, which could be well over a quarter of a mile long and 250 feet deep. The net was suspended vertically in the water, the top attached to a floating cork line whilst the bottom was weighted down with a so-called 'lead line'. Iron rings were fastened at intervals beneath the lead lines. Once the fish had been encircled a steel hawser threaded through the rings was winched in, closing, or pursing, the bottom of the net under the tuna.

During the pursing operation and afterwards approximately fifty per cent of the net was hauled back onboard the fishing vessel through the power block. As this happened, some of the trapped dolphins tried to escape by diving to the bottom of the net, only to become entangled in the mesh and asphyxiated. The strong instinct to assist each other in adversity, and for mothers to remain with their calves, resulted in many of them being injured as the net was drawn in. Once a dolphin was caught, the others would remain close-by and would make little attempt to escape.

To the fishermen, hell-bent on pulling out of the sea as many tuna as they could, the panicking of the dolphins and the dead dolphins caught in the nets were a hindrance. Additional effort and labour, which could have been directed to hauling-in tuna, had to be deployed in extricating the wounded and dead animals from the nets and tossing them back into the sea.

The high mortality of dolphins associated with the tuna fishing went virually unnoticed to those outside the industry itself until it was brought to the attention of the American public by the publication of an article by William Perrin, who sailed with the tuna fleet for two seasons to study the taxonomy and behaviour of dolphins. The young scientist described how sometimes hundreds of porpoises were either suffocated or battered to death in the sacking up of a single set. He cited catastrophic sets in which over 1,000 dolphins were slaughtered. Extrapolating from his experiences he estimated that between 250,000 and 400,000 dolphins were being killed each year in the eastern tropical Pacific. He speculated that such a level of mortality could lead to the collapse of dolphin populations.

These revelations shocked scientists and conservationists alike. Their individual concern and remonstrations built up quickly into a tidal wave of protest which swept towards the US Congress in Washington.

As a result in 1972 the Marine Mammal Protection Act became law in the USA. It stated that *The incidental kill or serious injury of mammals permitted in the course of commercial fishing operations be reduced to insignificant levels approaching zero.*

At first the conservationists were pleased that they had been instrumental in obtaining a reprieve for the many dolphins who would otherwise have met their deaths at the hands of the tuna men. However their satisfaction was short lived. For it soon became apparent that the fishermen were prepared blatantly to ignore the law. For eighteen months the tuna lobby kept up an unremitting pressure on the government to exempt 'incidental taking' of porpoises from the act. At the same time the fishermen researched methods of reducing the dolphin kill by modification of their nets and techniques.

Although the introduction of a large mesh section, called a Medina Panel, into the net considerably reduced the dolphin mortality it certainly did not eliminate deaths altogether. It was predicted in mid 1974 that the total porpoise deaths for the season would be about 100,000—hardly an insignificant level approaching zero. Many conservation groups joined in the bitter fight inside and outside the government to bring the tuna fishing industry to its senses. For apart from the tragedy of the slaughter of the dolphins, it seemed obvious to everyone, except the recalcitrant fishermen, that if they continued as they were doing, they would destroy the markers that enabled them to spot their valuable source of income.

When a group of conservationists take on an organisation with the formidable back-up of a government department, it is a David and Goliath contest from the start. The tuna industry claimed that a porpoise quota would bring the industry to its knees. They threatened to remove their boats and fish under foreign flags rather than have regulations forced upon them. Despite such protests the National Marine Fisheries Service established a quota of 52,000 dolphin mortalities for 1978 and 41,000 for 1979. As it turned out the death tolls were well below this, indicating that it is possible to catch tuna and not kill so many dolphins using modified purse seine method.

The American fishermen are disgruntled when they hear of fishermen of other nationalities catching tuna unimpeded by US regulations and quotas. With huge investments still being made in tuna boats in many parts of the world, it is sad to contemplate the ravages each vessel will inflict on the Pacific dolphin population whose cumulative incidental deaths at the hands of the tuna fishermen already exceeds six millions.

To the Faroese fishermen the concern expressed by many people to the plight of dolphins is hard for them to understand. The reason for their insensitivity is that for generations they have deliberately hunted a species of dolphin for food and continue to do so as their rightful harvest. However, they have become affluent like the rest of the western world, and there is now a considerable element of sport in their dolphin hunts. When he visited the islands in 1980, the undersea explorer Gordon Ridley got the impression that the men on these remote islands continue their tradition more for the benefit of the masculine image than for the food it provides.

The species of dolphin which suffers as the result of their predation is the Pilot whale (*Globicephala melaena*). The Pilot whale drives, or Grindadraps as they are called by the Faroese, are carried out in small open fishing boats. On sighting a school, the fishermen take to their boats and drive the dolphins slowly towards a convenient bay. Once they have been coralled close to a chosen shallow, the school is panicked by striking the hindmost dolphin on the tail. The Pilot whales then rush onto the beach where they are stranded and then killed by a knife cut through the neck into the spinal cord. The local sheriff subsequently arranges the distribution of the meat and blubber in accordance with a complex tradition.

An expedition to the Faroe Islands from Cambridge University in 1978 reported three Pilot whale drives which accounted for 611 deaths. In addition seventy Killer whales were driven ashore and killed. The Faroese also shot White-sided and White-beaked dolphins plus Common porpoises as well as illegally harpooning Fin whales.

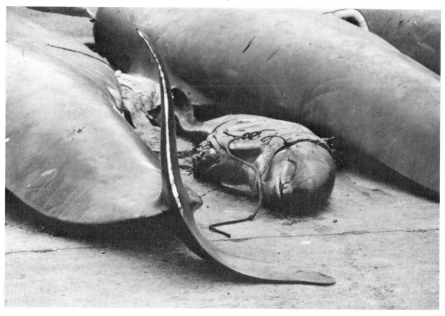

An aborted calf lies alongside its dead mother after a grindadrap in the Faroe Islands.

Gordon Ridley.

It was against this kind of background that a plan slowly took shape in my mind. Somehow or other I wanted to make people aware that dolphins could bring great joy into human lives. I took my inspiration from a completely unrelated field—that of ornithology.

Most of our knowledge on bird populations and migrations has come, not from professionals, but from amateur bird watchers, who ringed birds and recorded their observations. In doing so many of those involved developed a passion for the animals they studied. Bird watching provided untold hours of pleasure for thousands of people from all walks of life.

Furthermore, the Royal Society for the Protection of Birds grew in stature over the years and gained immense political power both in Britain and overseas. It had been responsible for safeguarding the habitats of birds. Thus birds, which would have been forced out of existence, were still part of the British urban and rural scene for those with eyes to see them.

I felt sure that the same could be done for the dolphins of the world. It was a much more difficult project. Firstly, because only those at sea or by the sea could participate and, secondly, because dolphins only presented themselves on the surface of the sea intermittently making accurate identification difficult. However, I knew that friends of mine who were birdwatchers could identify a bird from its characteristic flight pattern and shape. I felt sure dolphin watchers could do likewise. I decided to call my proposed scheme The Dolphin Survey Project and I formulated plans for recruiting an army of amateur dolphin spotters.

At the same time I conceived an even more ambitious project—one that would cover far wider aspects of delphinology. I eventually decided upon the title of INTERNATIONAL DOLPHIN WATCH and described its aims as: 'A programme to increase our knowledge and understanding of dolphins.'

Having decided upon my objectives, the next hurdle was how to make such a grandiose scheme work. To collect and analyse data gathered from all over the world in the Dolphin Survey Project, I needed to collaborate with a person or persons who could process the data. Ideally, my collaborator would be in a university department and have access to a computer.

A look through the scientific literature indicated that Richard Harrison stood head and shoulders above all others when it came to academic studies on cetaceans. In addition to being a Fellow of the Royal Society, which is certainly the most prestigious scientific body in Britain, if not in the world, Richard Harrison was Professor of Anatomy at the University of Cambridge.

I visited Professor Harrison and we were soon engrossed in an animated discussion on many aspects of dolphin behaviour. To me it was a delight to have the opportunity to meet a man who was both knowledgeable and enthusiastic about his subject.

Richard Harrison told me of his concern about the pollution of the seas and that he thought the build-up of high levels of chlorinated hydrocarbons derived from pesticides in the bodies of dolphins could be a contributory factor to the decrease in the dolphin population.

Professor Harrison confirmed that the dolphin population was on a strong downward trend. With dolphins living perhaps as long as forty years in the sea, the build-up over a period of time of toxic chemicals in their bodies could lead to circumstances which did not result in immediate death. This was an area with which I was familiar, because I had been involved for ten years in similar research. Indeed, I had personally presented papers on work carried out in my laboratory to meetings of The European Society for the Study of Drug Toxicity.

Professor Harrison said there were enormous gaps in our knowledge of dolphins and this applied particularly to their behaviour in the wild. When I described to him my concept of using amateur observers to gather information and suggested the production of a guide book or notes he said he already had such a project under way and would be pleased for me to progress it. When I was shown a series of paintings by one of his colleagues, Dennis McBrearty, of the twelve species of dolphins found around the British Coast, I realised I had been right to make contact with Cambridge University. We agreed a plan for co-operation in which we would pool our respective resources and talents. As Professor Harrison showed me out, his last words to me were 'I have been waiting thirty years for someone like you to come along.

For my part I could not have wished for a better arrangement. I was thrilled with the outcome of our meeting and eager to get to work on the Dolphin Survey Project which had become the major project under the umbrella title of International Dolphin Watch (IDW) which also covered my other dolphin interests.

IDW started to succeed from the moment the idea first came to me. Almost everyone I approached said they thought IDW was a good thing and would help if they could. I realised that this success would bring with it a much bigger work load than I could carry on my own, and my wife Wendy suggested I should approach the Manpower Services Commission (MSC)—which existed to help people find employment. Through the MSC I was told of a Special Temporary Employment Scheme (STEP) whereby I could obtain full-time help for the management of International Dolphin Watch, and that the state would finance the post for a period of one year. Thus I was able to recruit Elaine Orr, a newly qualified honours graduate who was unemployed and once again it seemed that the face of fortune was smiling upon IDW because she proved to be ideally suited to the post in every way.

One of the local resources in the village of North Ferriby, which was our base, was a printing works. It was run by a friend Jim Freeman, who

Our handbook has enabled many sailors to identify the dolphins they encountered on their voyages.

had given up full-time employment to set up his own small business in two unused rooms on the platform of the railway station. The railway was still in regular use and we discussed the production of a dolphin handbook to the sound of the printing press and the occasional train which rattled through the station. Jim suggested that before we embarked on a book we should consider publishing a broadsheet which would illustrate all of the dolphins on a single page. This idea met with the prompt approval of Professor Harrison. The poster gave us an immediate springboard from which to launch our recruitment campaign. International Dolphin Watch was underway.

6 TAKE ME TO THE DOLPHINS

DOLPHINS SHOULD BE FREE was the message boldly proclaimed at the foot of a letter I received from South Africa shortly after the launch of International Dolphin Watch. It came from Nan Rice the honorary secretary of The Dolphin Action and Protection Group.

A few months later my wife Wendy and I were winging our way to Cape Town to meet a group of conservationists who were dedicated to preserving the dolphin populations in their natural environment—the sea. We discovered Nan Rice to be a charming and very dynamic person. She and her colleagues organised a series of events and meetings for us which stimulated a lot of interest in dolphins and provided a more exciting overseas launch for International Dolphin Watch than I had dared to hope for.

My visit to South Africa brought to light several new dolphin stories. One of them pointed very clearly to the nature of the special bond that can exist between humans and dolphins. The Dolphin Action and Protection Group were opposed to the capture of dolphins for exhibition purposes But by one of those cruel twists of fate the story I am about to tell you is centred around the friendship of a young woman with captive dolphins.

I met Anne Rennie in Port Elizabeth. She was tiny in stature, less than five feet tall, and very smartly dressed in modern clothes. From what she told me later it was apparent that her almost frail appearance belied a tough lady. Her manner was vivacious and her eyes sparkled when she launched into animated discussion. She gestured with her hands as she talked, and her quick movements were those of a sensitive, emotional person.

It was December 1978, but Anne Rennie's story began over a decade earlier, shortly after two female Bottlenose dolphins were introduced into the Port Elizabeth dolphinarium. The unlikely names given to the two new inmates were those of well-known brands of Scotch whisky—Haig and Dimple. At the time Haig and Dimple came into her life Anne Rennie, the mother of two young children, was in the bloom of youthful womanhood. She was fast becoming an expert skindiver and was allowed into the pool with the newly-captured dolphins.

When Anne first lowered herself into the water, she began by swimming the 'dolphin stroke', with her hands at her side and kicking her feet up and down in unison. Haig—the younger of the two dolphins was intrigued by the nymph who had come into her pool. When the newcomer did corkscrew swims, stood on her head on the bottom of the pool, and carried out every manoeuvre she could invent in the gravity-free under-water world of the aqualung diver, the young female dolphin was de-lighted and followed Anne around the pool watching her every move. In contrast Dimple, the elder of the two dolphins, kept her distance, and watched disdainfully from afar. Anne tried to touch the dolphin who was obviously interested in her new human playmate. But whenever the diver extended her hand, Haig somehow managed to position herself just out of reach.

When Anne left the water she was enthralled with the friendship she had established with Haig. Visits to the dolphin pool became regular events. Haig joined in the games, but try as she would Anne could not touch the dolphin. Anne decided not to force the relationship with Haig and enjoyed just being with the dolphins and swimming in their company. Throughout all of these antics Dimple kept well clear. Although she was aloof Anne felt that the older dolphin secretly enjoyed the human addition to the pool.

Anne told me that a significant step forward was made in her relationship with the dolphins when physical contact was eventually established. Much to Anne's surprise it was Haig who took the initiative and started rubbing against her lady-friend.

Once the barrier between Anne and Haig was down it was not long before they had evolved new games which both of them enjoyed. Anne would hold onto Haig's dorsal fin and be towed round the pool. Alternatively Anne would put her hands in the mouth of the dolphin who would clench them gently between her teeth, like a horse bridle, before towing her human playmate around the dolphinarium. Not all of the towing was done by the dolphin however. Sometimes Anne would take the tail under her arms and tow the dolphin, who was much bigger than her, backwards around the pool. The two also developed a unique and extraordinary game in which the dolphin appeared to faint, and with eyes closed would drift to the bottom of the pool like a falling leaf. Anne would then dive down, pick up the dolphin in her arms as if she were cradling a child, and lift Haig, who remained limp, up to the surface.

Dimple watched these goings-on with a matronly detachment and would never become involved herself.

Anne Rennie with the dolphins who were later to help her through a very critical stage in her life.

Eastern Province Herald.

'Haig was the show-off,' said Anne Rennie. 'She was the one who did all of the leaps in the shows. Dimple always kept in the background. If Dimple came near me Haig would chase her away.'

Then one day the bond between Anne Rennie and Haig was forcibly broken. It happened when the two female dolphins were transferred to a larger pool in the company of a newly captured full-grown male called Daan who quickly established himself as the dominant dolphin. When Anne went into the pool to play with Haig, Daan immediately interfered. When they continued to associate, he made it quite clear to both of his female subordinates that he would not tolerate their close playful relationship. He threatened both of them, beat them with his tail fluke and raked them with his teeth.

'I was very upset,' said Anne continuing her story.

'You know if I was miserable or unhappy, I would go into the pool. And, after playing with Haig, I would come out absolutely bursting with joy. Haig lit something inside me and eliminated all of the bad things.'

I was to find out the following day just how utterly sincere Anne was when she made this statement.

'What happened next?' I enquired.

'Daan was quite fearless and allowed me to touch him from the start. So I played the games with him.'

'Did you play the same games with Daan that you did with Haig?' I questioned.

'Yes, exactly,' she said. 'He'd go to the surface and faint. Fall to the bottom. This big lump—850 pounds—really big, would lie on the bottom. Now I weigh 102 pounds and I'd go down and get on my hands and knees and take him to the surface with his dorsal fin between my arms. He'd be dead—his eyes closed. Get to the surface, he'd shiver, and down to the bottom he would go again. And God, you'd have to go down and pick him up again.'

Anne explained that she had never worn gloves when she played with Haig. Then she showed me some scars on her hands and told me how they came about.

'I went and stroked his mouth for the first time. He grabbed my hand and shook it like a rag doll. It was in tatters.'

This might have caused a lesser person to give up playing with the dolphins—but not Anne Rennie. She decided to take on the huge Daan, who was eight times her weight and could have destroyed her in seconds if he so wished. She did take the precaution of wearing gloves. I asked her how she dealt with him when he hit her with his tail or bit her.

'I used to sock him. Then ignore him. After a few moments he'd come and snuggle up against me. In the end I couldn't resist him. He was the most delightful character you could ever wish to find.'

And so it was that Anne Rennie was compelled to transfer her attentions to the dominant male dolphin—who enchanted her—and for whom she developed an even stronger relationship than that which existed between herself and Haig.

Our discussions ranged over many aspects of dolphin behaviour and included the mysterious quality which dolphins have of making people feel happy and even helping them in times of mental stress. We talked for hours and when we parted company I had a slight suspicion there was something more to come to light in Anne Rennie's story. Something deep down which she could not bring herself to talk about. We agreed to meet for lunch the following day. It was a day for a special celebration as it was the tenth birthday of Daan's daughter Dolly.

Anne arrived on time outside the dolphinarium bearing a scrap book full of press cuttings and photographs of her with Haig and Dimple. She had obviously attracted quite a lot of attention at the time, and it was not difficult to see why. She was beautiful. People like to see pretty girls in their newspapers and when they can be photographed alongside animals with as much appeal as dolphins the editor knows he's onto a winner.

We sat turning the pages in the heat of the mid-day sun. Anne became emotional as the curtains were pulled back on images that had been hidden in her subconscious mind. When she saw pictures of Daan tears started to stream down her face and she told me how the dolphins had helped her get through a tremendous emotional crisis in her life.

It started with her simply being embarrassed when she began to discharge blood when she was swimming. She went to her doctor who examined her and told her that she had cancer of the womb and would have to be operated on immediately.

The effect that such a diagnosis would have on a sensitive woman with a young family is not difficult to imagine. The fact that cancer, in one form or another, gives rise to so many deaths causes the very word cancer to strike horror in many people. Anne was stricken with fear and apprehension. When she heard the news, she was so bemused she could not face the prospect of telling anyone—even her husband. There was one thought in her mind.

'Take me to the dolphins,' she pleaded.

She went straightway to the dolphinarium and played with the dolphins. As she did so the burden of the frightening news became tolerable and she gathered together the fragments of her shattered peace of mind. When she left the dolphinarium she was able to face-up to the future and was in a fit mental state to break the news to her family. That mysterious force which seems to spring from dolphins helped Anne to ride the worst storm in her young life. The fact that she was alive ten years later was evidence of the complete success of the surgical operation.

Nobody goes through that kind of experience without it having a profound effect. And nobody, not even Anne herself, will fully realise how it changed her attitude towards life and her relationships with those around her. She seldom went back into the dolphinarium after her recovery. It was as if one chapter in her life had been completed and it was time to turn a new page.

Anne told us her story outside the dolphinarium. She declined to go inside. When she walked away, with her scrapbook under her arm, I knew she had no doubt in her mind that the dolphins had helped her to survive a crisis. The memories of that most difficult time in her life were still painful ten years later.

7 DEATH ON THE BEACH

Once International Dolphin Watch was launched, details of dolphin sightings arrived at my home often from unexpected and surprising sources. Not all were of dolphins swimming joyfully free in the sea. The events which followed one such report developed into a deeply distressing situation for me.

It happened on a Sunday 18 March 1979. The news of a stranded dolphin was 'phoned through to some friends in Harrogate with whom my wife and I were spending the day. It was snowing hard and when we set off I wondered if we would be able to make the journey to Spurn Point where the dolphin—which had been named Spurn—was stranded. As our home was en route for the coast we called in to collect my wellington boots plus our children Ashley and Melanie, and we left immediately for Spurn Head, about thirty miles away.

It was the coastguards who had first spotted the stranded dolphin on the previous afternoon. With the aid of the lifeboat crew, they got the dolphin back into the water as the incoming tide crept slowly and gently inshore to cover the mud flats. The following morning, however, they found the dolphin was once again lying stranded on the mud when the tide receded. With the aid of the local RSPCA officer they managed to get some sponge rubber mattresses under the dolphin, whose body was covered with a sack and kept regularly dowsed with water. The coast-guard then telephoned various contacts including me, and by mid-afternoon I drove into the bird sanctuary at Spurn to see what assistance I could give.

The White-sided dolphin was fully grown and appeared to be in good condition apart from some superficial wounds which were bleeding, and a small abscess on the tail stock, which looked as if it might have been caused by a small calibre bullet.

The profile of the head was similar to that of Donald, although Spurn's beak was less pronounced. The top of his head was grey, but the rostrum was creamy white with a distinct border between the two zones of colour. This gave the White-sided dolphin the look of a melancholy clown and the tears that streamed from Spurn's eyes added to his disconsolate appearance. He presented a very forlorn sight. His respiration was laboured and erratic. I opened his mouth and found that the conical teeth were in good condition. From this I concluded that the dolphin had not come ashore to die of old age.

The most logical explanation for his presence was that he had come into the bay of shallow tidal water and had been unable to find a way out through the maze of drainage channels that eventually led to the safety of deeper water. His head was pointing in the direction of the open sea, which was about 300 yards away on the other side of the long spit of sand that comprised Spurn Head. One of the onlookers suggested that the dolphin could hear the sound of the waves on the far shore and that he had beached himself in an attempt to reach the open sea, not knowing that there was a barrier of sand between them.

The watery sun, which occasionally appeared through the slightly misty air casting a yellow band across the still water in the bay, was sinking. There were a few hours of daylight left, and it was getting colder.

The author, right, confirms that Spurn is a White-sided dolphin from the International Dolphin Watch chart.

Ashley Dobbs.

What could we do? We could wait for the tide to come in again and hope that the dolphin would swim free and find his way back into the Humber Estuary and thence out into the open sea. The events of the day before had shown that this was unlikely to be a successful solution to the problem. An alternative was to wait for a crew which had set off from the dolphinarium at Woburn. They were not expected to arrive for several hours and, even if the dolphin survived the long journey back to the pool, that was no guarantee that Spurn would live long in captivity. As I stood

The dolphin stranded on thick mud at Spurn Head had a disconsolate appearance.

Ashley Dobbs.

looking down at the dolphin wondering how I could help, I heard the sound of the waves scurrying up the beach which was out of sight just behind me. As I looked at the immobile dolphin at my feet I could not help thinking of Donald and his obvious love of life in the open sea. The best chance Spurn had of regaining his freedom was for me to find some way of getting the dolphin across the 300 yards of mud flats and sand dunes that separated him from the open sea. I had to make an attempt to get the dolphin into deep water.

I estimated Spurn's weight to be between 400 and 500 pounds and he was extremely difficult to manoeuvre because he had stranded in an area of thick black glutinous mud into which our feet sank. I quickly found some boards along the high water mark and these were placed around the dolphin. After a great deal of struggling, we managed to get a canvas sheet under him. We were aided by some of the sightseers and by John Chichester-Constable who had Seignorian rights and was responsible to the Crown for dealing with all 'Royal Fish' which landed between the high and low water marks on the foreshore between Flamborough Head and Spurn Point.

It was a long hard struggle, but with the front of the sling roped to a Land Rover we heaved the dolphin across the soft sand. We lifted him over the track running down the centre of the sand spit and moved him round the posts and obstacles that obstructed our route to the open sea. At last we were on the beach, which was of course gravel. Within a few minutes we had the dolphin at the water's edge. It was at this stage that what should have been triumph turned into tragedy.

The direct cause of this unfortunate turn of events was the surf that came creaming up the beach with every wave. Out to sea the waves were two to three feet high. As they came towards the shore the crests raced ahead until they broke away turning into a mass of frothy water that rushed up the shore pulling the shingle with it. Thus when each wave was near the limit of its travel it was not a body of buoyant water. Instead it consisted of air, water and stones that acted like a pump, pushing anything in its path up the beach. When each wave exhausted itself the pebbles were deposited, the air bubbles dispersed, and just the water flowed back into the sea, carrying with it only lightweight objects that would easily float.

We got the dolphin to the foaming edge of the sea. The people who had helped us so valiantly during the past hour were weary and were thankful to relieve themselves of the burden. In addition to myself only a couple of people, including John Chichester-Constable, were wearing wellington boots. Thus it was left to us to carry the dolphin on the final short leg of his journey back into the sea.

We managed to drag the dolphin into the shallow surf but as the sea came rushing in we were abandoned by those who did not want to get their shoes full of water. Also the sun had long since disappeared and it was getting decidedly colder in the misty fading light. So the prospect of wet feet was not a pleasant one.

As the first wave of foam swept over the lower part of the dolphin, he seemed to be injected with a spirit to survive. His respiration became sharp and regular and Spurn thrashed with his tail as if trying to swim. But it was to no avail. He remained firmly where he was.

When the next wave swept in, it was higher than the previous one. It curled over the tops of our boots, which were instantly filled with sea water. But worse still, it pushed the dolphin back a short way despite our desperate attempts to hold the dolphin against the surge. When the wave had passed, we tried to manoeuvre the dolphin forward with the backrush of water. Spurn tried to help himself by thrashing his tail. But it had nothing but air to react against and the dolphin could generate no propulsive force. When the wave receded, we were left with the dolphin on the beach and our boots full of water. After several more fruitless attempts to get the dolphin into deep water, Mr Chichester-Constable, who was by this time wet to the knees, admitted that he was recovering from influenza and felt that it was not provident to continue to expose himself to the cold water any more.

So my son Ashley and my daughter Melanie, neither of whom had come prepared with wellington boots, valiantly waded into the water and tried to help me move the dolphin forward. Inch by inch we made progress forward as the waves receded and just managed to stop the dolphin being swept back towards the shore with each inrush of water. Then a large wave rushed in. It spun the dolphin sideways. I tried to stop it by pushing my feet hard into the sand and gravel. But such was the force on the dolphin that I was bowled over. Melanie and Ashley managed to stay upright but had water nearly up to their waists. As I stumbled, Spurn was swept past me and carried back and dumped high up the beach despite his efforts to swim free. As the sea receded he slithered a few feet back towards the sea and stopped. When the wave spent itself, the dolphin was left like a piece of driftwood on the tide line.

Spurn was bleeding from abrasions he had received on the gravel and he presented a piteous sight. I realised that there was nothing more we could do for him except hope that he might be carried back to the sea by another large wave. But that was a forlorn hope and I knew it.

The air temperature was ice cold, it was almost dark and the three of us were utterly exhausted. All of the sightseers and helpers had gone except for one officer of the RSPCA.

We had no dry clothes to change into and we were saturated with sea water. I emptied the water out of my wellington boots and put the sodden shoes belonging to Melanie and Ashley in the boot of the car. We were all cold, wet, uncomfortable and dejected when we set off on the thirty mile

We managed to make a stretcher onto which we moved the dolphin.
Ashley Dobbs.

journey back home. On the car radio we heard that many roads in the nearby Wolds were still completely blocked by snow, but fortunately we were spared the ordeal of having to drive home through a blizzard. But the vision of a lonely dolphin being tossed up the beach like a piece of driftwood remained with me and I have been haunted by it many times since.

The following day I learned that the team from the dolphinarium carried Spurn back to Woburn where he was covered with Vaseline and tended through the night by Jackie Wyatt. Sadly the dolphin died the following morning.

8   HUNT THE DOLPHIN

The chances of a diver seeing a wild friendly dolphin swimming free in the sea are extremely remote. So when Chris Gooson, my partner with whom I made underwater films, telephoned me to say he had just seen a wild dolphin in the Red Sea I got him to tell me the full story.

Chris explained that he had been to Ras Muhammed with a BBC producer Duncan Gibbins. Chris and I had become firm friends with Duncan with whom we had enjoyed several assignments. Having filmed a Greek freighter carrying china clay which had gone aground and threatened to destroy the underwater paradise, the two divers decided to have a last dive at Coral Island on the way back to Eilat. And Chris, not wishing to lose an opportunity to get some more shots for a television movie we were making about the Red Sea, took the camera in with him. They were in the company of a very experienced Dutch diver, named Paul, who found an octopus amongst the coral heads and pursuaded it to leave its lair. Whereupon the disgruntled octopus attached itself firmly with its suckers to the Dutch diver's facemask and mouthpiece. After Chris filmed this unexpected turn of events he was aware of another presence. He glanced round and to his utter amazement there was a six foot long dolphin just a few feet away watching the spectacle.

At this point the octopus decided it was time to leave the scene and swam away from Paul leaving a cloud of ink in the water.

'The dolphin completely ignored the octopus and seemed to be watching Paul,' Chris said.

Chris, Duncan and Paul followed the dolphin down into the depths. Chris had fifty feet of film left in his camera. He focused the lens and had just started to shoot when there was a deafening roar. He looked up through the clear water and could see the hull of a large boat overhead.

'A huge anchor and chain came hurtling down into the water just a few feet away and the engines were put into full reverse.'

Chris was furious, not because of the danger, but because he thought the noise would frighten the dolphin away.

Everything then went quiet and a host of people wearing fins, masks and snorkels jumped into the sea from the big boat. Much to the surprise of Chris the dolphin ignored the overhead activity. Instead the dolphin stayed with the divers until distracted by a new activity overhead.

A couple jumped into the water with aqualungs. The girl was bronzed and wearing only the pants of a very brief bikini. The dolphin swam slowly up and circled round the new arrivals and then descended again to a depth of fifty feet. Then suddenly the dolphin hurtled towards the surface. Such was the clarity of the water in the Red Sea that Chris could see the dolphin's grey shape above the sea before it plunged back in again.

Chris watched the dolphin rocket towards the surface through the viewfinder of his underwater camera.

Horace Dobbs.

'It was the most incredible jump,' reported Chris. 'He must have leapt a tremendous height out of the water. The remora fish that was earlier clinging to his back was just hanging on near the dolphin's tail.'

The dolphin then made two more jumps in quick succession. This time Chris was ready for the action and watched it through the viewfinder as the last feet of film ran through the camera. After his third show of aerial acrobatics the dolphin stayed with those snorkellers who had not rushed back onboard the boat. Chris and his companions rose closer to the surface and watched the ballet of movements over their heads.

'Then everybody climbed back onboard,' continued Chris. 'And the dolphin followed the boat as it sailed away.'

Although Chris was overjoyed at the experience of diving with the dolphin, he was disappointed that he had only a small amount of film left in the camera. He and Duncan were scheduled to fly home the following day and had to be at Eilat Airport at noon. Although diving on the same day as flying is not recommended because of the increased risk of bends, the two divers decided they could safely get another shallow dive with the dolphin before their departure.

By 9.30 the next morning Chris, Duncan and Paul were kitted and back in the sea off Coral Island. The divers made every kind of underwater noise they could think of to attract the dolphin—but he didn't turn up. At the end of the dive Chris decided to use the film in his camera and the party set off underwater for the long swim back to shore. When they were just a few feet from land, Chris looked up. The dolphin was just five feet away. There was no time to change the film. But there was time to have a brief swim with the unpunctual dolphin.

As soon as he arrived back in England Chris telephoned me. We were planning to make a TV programme on dolphins in addition to our Red Sea film. So I had a ready-made excuse to suggest that we should return to Eilat.

I had no sooner put the 'phone down when it rang again. The next caller was Duncan Gibbins. Duncan could not have sounded more excited if he had discovered a goldmine.

'You should have seen him, Horace,' he blurted out lapsing into one of the many colourful dialects with which he embroidered his verbal pictures.

'He was fooking fantastic. It blew poor auld Goosen's mind,' he said, in a stage Irish accent, grossly exaggerating the hint of Irish intonation that gave away my partner's homeland.

Duncan knew of my failure to meet Sandy in the Bahamas and when I told him I was planning to go back with Chris he could not conceal his envy.

'You lucky buggers,' he said in broad Cockney. 'You know I'd really piss myself if you didn't find him,' he added in a mischievous voice.

I loudly retorted that there was not the remotest chance that a dolphin

Just as Chris was about to leave the water the dolphin appeared cheekily alongside.

Horace Dobbs.

would allow him so much selfish pleasure. However, from my experience in the Bahamas I knew that finding a wild dolphin in the sea could be even more of a risky business than searching for sunken treasure.

Exactly one week later Chris and I were together on a plane bound for Eilat. With us was his wife Jill.

Immediately we arrived in Eilat we made our way to the Aqua-sport dive centre at Coral Beach. We needed a check-out dive. I wanted to drive immediately to Coral Island which was about seven miles away, but Chris thought it better to do a much easier dive from the beach as Jill had not been under the sea for about a year. He also pointed out that we had six days in which we could enjoy the company of the dolphin. Reluctantly I conceded.

The following morning we were back at the diving centre as soon as it opened to make arrangements for a boat to act as surface support for our dives at Coral Island.

Some time later, with the vessel well laden with our cameras, lights and diving gear, we were underway for Coral Island, and our rendezvous with the dolphin.

When we arrived it appeared that nobody had informed the dolphin of his appointment with us. The boatman, named Ellie, who ferried passengers from the mainland to the island told us that the dolphin had been there the previous evening but had not yet turned up.

Chris was absolutely confident that the dolphin would come to us once we were in the water. So we anchored over a wreck at exactly the same spot where the encounters had taken place one week earlier. With cameras loaded and at the ready we went overboard excited and expectant, anticipating that the dolphin would be attracted by the sound of our bubbles. For fifteen minutes we swam amongst the giant coral heads occasionally calling out into the water. But no dolphin.

When I studied Donald off the British coast, I quickly discovered that I could call him up by making sharp sounds. I estimated he would come from several miles away if I used my aqualung cylinder as a kind of underwater gong. So I tried the same trick under the Red Sea and tapped the base of my air tank with the metal handle of my diving knife. The sound radiated into the water. When the dolphin still failed to turn up, we continued to call and tap as we glided down deeper. Away from the bright shallows, we journeyed into a horizonless world filled with diffuse blue light. We were weightless travellers on a journey through the huge inner space of the ocean waiting for the arrival of a small spaceship, shaped like a dolphin. But our hoped-for rendezvous with the alien intelligence did not take place. Disappointed, but not too disheartened, we made our way back to the boat without shooting a single frame of film.

Chris was convinced that the Dutchman, Paul, had a special way with the dolphin. The following day we agreed to meet Paul at Coral Island and use his magnetic power to attract our quarry. But that did not work either.

In the evening we reviewed the situation. Two of our five full diving days had gone. When we discussed the matter with Paul we discovered that he had dived with the dolphin on only four occasions and one of these was with Chris. The other three were widely spaced over a period of several months. We questioned everyone who might give us clues in our dolphin hunt. Those who had dived with the dolphin were ecstatic about him. This included Willy Halpert who described how he and other divers found their underwater encounters with the dolphin to be some of the most exhilarating experiences in the thousands of hours spent under the sea.

'When did you see him?' I enquired when I could find a gap in the commentary.

'On Saturday, one day after Chris left for England.'

Further detective work showed that on the first day of our visit to Coral Island the dolphin had put in a brief appearance at Raffi Nelson's Village — a place between Coral Island and Eilat.

'That means we could actually have sailed right past him on our way to Coral Island,' I said to Chris who had already reached the same obvious conclusion.

We worked out a new plan of campaign and agreed that we would have to do much more reconnaissance before rushing to Coral Island.

Day three was a very bad day. It was excessively hot. In the shade the temperature reached 130°F (55°C); exposed directly to the sun it was even higher. The wind was blowing and standing outside was like being in the path of a giant hair dryer.

We knew the dangers of dehydration in such climatic conditions. We were sitting on the terrace at the diving centre, having a last drink before launching the boat, when I was told that there was an urgent message waiting for me at the Caravan Hotel where we were staying.

'Someone's seen the dolphin,' I shouted to Chris as I jumped up and ran across the road to the hotel opposite — convinced that one of our contacts was reporting in.

It was a message from a Telex machine very faintly typed in red. I scanned it quickly. It was not about dolphins at all. I tried to read it but my eyes were filling with tears and my legs felt as if they had suddenly turned to rubber. Only certain words registered—RING HOME URGENTLY ... DAUGHTER ... TAKEN TO HOSPITAL ... BRAIN DAMAGE ... ATTACKED BY MODS.

I held on to the counter to steady myself and tried to read it properly, but the words fused into a pink blur. I picked up the insignificant-looking piece of buff paper and stumbled across the road to find Chris. I laid it on the table and asked him to read it to me.

He smoothed the crumpled paper out with his hands and read it through a couple of times. Then he looked up and said. 'It's not Melanie who has been attacked. It's her boyfriend.'

When I had regained my composure and Chris re-read the message out loud the meaning was obvious. Even so it was some minutes before I felt in a fit state to return to the hotel and telephone England.

When I spoke to my wife Wendy, she informed me that Melanie's boyfriend Don had gone out with some of his pals to a club in Hull to celebrate the end of exams and the fact that he was to become officially engaged to my daughter on the following day. When he and a friend left they were jumped on from behind. In addition to suffering a blow to the head which had produced a four inch fracture of the skull the boy had been kicked in the face and ribs. As far as Wendy could find out there was no motive, only gratuitous violence. He was not robbed but left unconscious in the gutter with blood streaming from his head and that was how the police found him. When I spoke to her he was still unconscious, although he occasionally thrashed about violently in bed. My daughter, who was nursing him in hospital, was extremely distressed and was told by the specialist that it was impossible to predict at this stage whether there would be any permanent brain damage.

When I suggested I should fly home immediately she said there was nothing I could do. We could only wait and see what happened. We agreed that I should return home in three days time as scheduled, and we would keep in touch by telephone.

When Chris and I set off in the boat to find the dolphin the events in far-away England kept flashing on the screen of my mind like a horror movie.

We had become very friendly with the boatman on the ferry at Coral Island. He operated his small glassbottomed boat according to demand and was always one of the first people to know when the dolphin arrived. He agreed to keep constant watch whilst we scouted up and down the coast in the car. He was very hopeful that Wednesday would be the day, because he worked out that the dolphin was often away for periods of three days at a time. Thus he deduced the dolphin would be back at Coral Island on the fourth day of our five-day filming schedule.

The next day began as all of the others, with the sun rising into a pink sky that was soon transformed into unbroken blue. As it did so the temperature climbed from the eighties, through the hundred mark, and up on the Fahrenheit scale. We had decided to abandon the boat and concentrate on covering as much coastline as possible using the car. But at the end of the fourth day we were no nearer our goal. As the sun went down we watched Coral Island become a black silhouette against the faintly misty mountains of Jordan on the far side of the Gulf. They appeared to be only a short distance away. The trip across the Gulf certainly did not pose much of a journey to a dolphin to whom international boundaries were of no significance.

'You realise that he could be in Jordan,' I said to Chris as I sat transfixed by the vision of layer upon layer of distant mountains, slowly changing hues from pink to purple.

'I know,' he replied. 'If that's the case there is absolutely no way of us knowing where he is. And tomorrow is our last day.'

Our hopes of finding the dolphin faded with the sunset.

The next day we didn't hurry through breakfast. When the time came to carry the heavy engine and our diving and camera equipment down the beach to the boat we dallied, and after our labours in the hot sun we had an extra drink in the shade before setting off on the journey to Coral Island. On the way, I searched every quarter carefully with my binoculars, but there was nothing to signify the presence of our quarry. Thoughts of my fruitless trip to the Bahamas invaded my mind and they were coupled with visions of Duncan Gibbins convulsed with unsuppressed laughter.

We headed straight for the jetty. As we approached the ferryman, Ellie, rushed out of the restaurant waving his arms. He came running down to the edge of the pier as we were about to tie up.

'He's here! He's here!' he shouted waving his arms in triumph and as excited as if he had just shot a winning goal at a cup final.

'He was here at five o'clock this morning,' he blurted out. From what he said, we gathered he had tried everything in his power to get a message to us. But there was no 'phone, no taxi and he could not contact anybody going through to Eilat to carry a message. It was already late morning and we were working fast at getting ready. Then he electrified us further by saying, 'Hurry, hurry, he could go at any time.'

'Jill, you get in the water and keep the dolphin amused,' ordered Chris.

The boatman already had the engine of his ferry running and Jill, who was wearing a swimming costume, grabbed her mask and fins, jumped aboard whilst Chris and I frantically started to kit up with full diving equipment and cameras. The dolphin was in the middle of the channel between the island and the mainland. Jill soon splashed into the sea. We watched her submerge and the triangular dorsal fin of the dolphin move towards her.

Chris was convinced that the dolphin would swim to us once we were in the water. As soon as we were ready, we took our boat to the place where he had encountered the dolphin previously, which had the essential facility of a line to which we could moor. Chris was first in the water with his camera. A few moments later I too slid over the side. Chris was forty feet down tapping the metal wing of his camera housing with his knife and looking around. As I approached I could hear the sound but the dolphin was nowhere to be seen. I scoured the blue limit of my visibility.

Human-dolphin encounter off Coral Island in the Red Sea.

Horace Dobbs.

Then in the distance a grey shape appeared out of the mist like a ghost. I held my breath. There was complete silence. The dolphin continued to fly towards me. As he did so the diffuse shape materialised, until a very solid-looking dolphin was swimming just a few feet away. There was no hurry or excitement — the dolphin moved slowly past as if summing me up. The eye that was assessing me was half shut. I immediately got the feeling I was in the presence of a friendly, gentle creature. His approach was so smooth and peaceful I didn't feel immediate ecstatic excitement. I felt more as I might if I met-up with a friendly neighbour whilst walking to the shops. The presence of the dolphin felt absolutely normal. We swam

The dolphin swam up towards the bikinied bather on the surface.

Horace Dobbs.

slowly together side by side like two friends casually passing the time of day.

Then he cruised round gently and headed down towards Chris, who had his camera up to his mask and was filming our meeting.

Now it was my turn to film. Through the reflex viewfinder of my camera I watched the dolphin spiral down to Chris as if I was actually watching a film in slow motion. He swam through the curtain of rising air bubbles and circled round Chris. Then the dolphin swam towards one of the large bubbles and playfully bit at it, splitting it into a dozen small scintillating spheres that oscillated as they chased one another upwards.

I soon exposed the thirty metres of film in my 16mm. cine camera and returned to the boat to change the film. I had come prepared to spend many hours with the dolphin and I wanted to observe and record his responses to the same kind of objects and situations which had produced such interesting reactions in Donald. So, whilst I changed the film in my camera, Chris took the opportunity of taking down objects of different shapes and textures. These included a rubber quoit attached to stout fluorescent tape. On many occasions Donald had taken a quoit in his mouth and towed me through the water whilst I hung on to the line, Also Donald was fascinated by mechanical objects especially if they made a

Jill snorkelled down to join the dolphin.

Horace Dobbs.

noise. But the Coral Island dolphin showed no interest in them what-soever. And, when I played music and made other noises to him via my underwater loudspeaker, I noticed no response apart from a glancing look.

This dolphin appeared to be much more interested in people and what divers did. Chris pulled his hand into his chest and stuck his elbow out, attempting to imitate a dolphin's flipper. When Chris wagged his elbow rapidly the dolphin immediately responded by waving one of his flippers. When Chris then arched his body several times, the dolphin did likewise. All of the time the dolphin was watching Chris carefully as if encouraging him to invent a new game for their mutual amusement. When Chris rose to the surface and popped his head out of the water he was surprised to see the dolphin follow him up and do the same. Obviously the dolphin wanted to continue the game. So Chris bobbed up and down in the water and much to his amusement the dolphin did the same. From afar they looked as if they were on opposite ends of an underwater see-saw — with each of them breaking surface alternately. When that game was over and the diver swam away using the dolphin stroke, the dolphin swam in unison very close alongside. However, when Chris put his hand out to touch his playmate, the dolphin always remained just out of reach.

By the time Chris had exposed all of his film I was ready to go back in again. So too was Jill who had been picked up by the boatman from the middle of the channel. With Jill was another snorkel diver — an attractive young lady of French origin named Estelle. With beautiful girls and a dolphin for company I sank slowly into the transparent water. The sun shone and my bubbles glittered as they gurgled towards the ever-changing canopy of blue and silver over my head. The girls, who were not wearing underwater breathing apparatus snorkelled down towards the

A pair of white legs frantically pumping up and down looked comic from underwater when a family rushed into the sea to join the dolphin.
Horace Dobbs.

dolphin who weaved in an endless pattern of sweeps and curves through the water. From below it looked like an aerial ballet.

Unfettered by gravity, my bikinied ballerinas were able to fly and twirl through the water for as long as they could hold their breath. I was the only member of the audience in the underwater stalls to appreciate the show.

The dolphin ballet come to an abrupt end when a family group on the island decided to go for a swim. The dolphin disappeared. When I surfaced and heard shrieks of excitement coming from afar I knew immediately the source of their thrills. The dolphin was obviously amongst them. So in the company of the two deserted underwater ballerinas I swam off to join the fun.

When we arrived there was much splashing. The youngsters were bobbing down, swimming frantically underwater for a few seconds and then popping up again. Estelle also started to rush after the dolphin, stretching out her arms towards him. However the bra of her bikini was not designed for such vigorous exertions and she briefly joined the ranks

Several times the dolphin swam to the bottom and pushed his forehead against the same small coral head. We never found out why he did this.

Horace Dobbs.

of the topless maidens who adorned many of Eilat's beaches. The dolphin, however, gave her no more than a passing glance.

When Chris came back into the water the snorkellers went back to shore. The dolphin stayed with us and we had time to look at him in detail as he cruised slowly round. I saw his teeth only very briefly and they appeared to be in good condition. So I guessed he was a young adult.

There was one aspect of the dolphin's behaviour for which we could find no explanation. He would descend to the bottom and press his forehead (called the melon) against a small coral head. We watched him

Jill and the dolphin both moved gracefully under the sea.

Horace Dobbs.

do this several times and on each occasion he always used the same piece of coral, although there were several similar outcrops close-by to choose from.

After spending nearly three hours in the water, I climbed aboard our boat to recover, whilst Chris reloaded our cine cameras onshore. When I did so the dolphin swam slowly away. When Chris returned, I had revived sufficiently to go back into the water. Jill and Estelle, who had also taken a breather jumped in with us, but try as we might we could not attract the dolphin back.

Although we stayed in the water for some time, we reached the conclusion that our cetacean playmate had gone. We headed back for base.

We had aroused tremendous interest in our quest for the dolphin. Wherever we went people would enquire about our success. When we got back to the diving centre in Eilat that night I felt like an olympic athlete returning home with a gold medal.

Yes, we had met the dolphin. Yes, we had a fantastic time with him. Yes, we had filmed him. Yes, we had taken stills and cine.

There had always been some doubt about what species he was, and I was able to answer Willy Halpert's next question.

'He's a Bottlenose dolphin' I told him.

'Male or female?' asked Willy.

'Definitely male.'

Willy was obviously delighted to hear this because my statements confirmed his somewhat diffident identification.

'Have you got a name for him?' he continued, with a bright sparkle in his deep brown eyes.

'Well as a matter of fact, no — although I have some ideas,' I retorted.

'Well don't bother,' said Willy. 'I just wanted you to confirm that he was male.'

'Come on Willy,' I jibed. 'Out with it. What name have you dreamed-up?'

'Dobbie,' he replied, beaming.

We were due to fly out of Eilat at twelve o'clock the following day and hoped that we would be able to have two encounters with the dolphin on successive days. But it was not to be. We stayed in the water off Coral Island until the last possible moment before rushing to the airport. We packed our still soggy wetsuits and our masses of camera equipment at the check-in desk. All in all it was a very impressive and very untidy load. If our rolls of exposed film had been made of platinum, they could not have been more valuable to us.

Less than twenty-four hours after our touch down in England, I had an excited call from Chris who had viewed the rushes.

'The footage is fantastic,' he enthused down the telephone.

'And we've denied old Gibbins the pleasure of pissing himself with laughter.'

Fortunately the incident which caused me so much anxiety had a happy ending. Don made a complete recovery from his terrible injuries. At the time of writing his plans for marriage to my daughter are well advanced.

Sadly, however, the story of Dobbie did not end in the same way. A few months after our visit I had a letter from a qualified biologist working at a marine biological laboratory in Eilat. He informed me that the body of a dolphin bearing very distinctive marks had been washed ashore.

Dobbie had been killed with a shot from a rifle.

9 UNDERSEA RAILROAD

When I first met Donald I felt there must be a special link between man and dolphins but I could not define it. When I encountered Dobbie in the Red Sea six years later, I had still not solved the conundrum, although I had lots more information and experiences to work with. I decided I had taken too broad a view and planned to review those cases where the human-dolphin connection was most strongly felt. I started with Nan Rice.

Nan Rice founded the Dolphin Action and Protection Group in May 1977, but her feelings were first aroused to high level in 1969 when on 21 December she saw Dusky dolphins being netted in Hout Bay. Two hundred dolphins were captured in order that six could be selected for exhibition in captivity. Some were wounded and died during the capture operation.

The wave of protest generated by Nan Rice and other witnesses did not go unheeded by the authorities, and their case was strengthened when one of the three newly captured dolphins died in Tygerberg Zoo on 14 January. Less than one week later all dolphins were declared protected mammals around the coast of South Africa.

In 1977 Dr Heydorn, Director of the Durban Oceanic Research Institute, had a meeting in Hout Bay and put forward a proposal that he catch eight Dusky dolphins—two for his oceanarium and six for export. Petitions against this catch were signed by hundreds of residents and others, resulting in the withdrawal of the permit.

Despite this public opposition, however, one year later a team from Durban appeared in Hout Bay to catch a mate for the lone Dusky dolphin in their oceanarium. Two females were caught close inshore and one of the dolphins died on the way to Durban. This death caused a furore which involved the newly formed Dolphin Action and Protection Group in an enormous amount of work and publicity. Many of the cars in the area were seen to bear stickers with their slogan: DOLPHINS SHOULD BE FREE.

Nan Rice and her colleagues of the Dolphin Action and Protection

Group were not alone in expressing these sentiments. In an article in the
Cape Times on 18 March 1978 entitled 'Dolphins and our changing
morality', Graham Ferreira balanced the arguments put to both sides and
compared them with two card players each trying to overtrump the other.
His conclusion was that Dr Heydorn's battle was not with the dolphin
protectionists, but with his own conscience. In a later article, Ferreira
looked at the morality of dolphin capture in the wider context of man's
relationship with his total environment and the coinhabitants of the
earth. He concluded that we could not have a healthy society in an
unhealthy environment, and added that it was about time this generation
stopped filling their pockets at the expense of the environment.

I added my own contribution to the debate when my wife and I visited
South Africa to launch International Dolphin Watch. After one of my
presentations in Hout Bay a member of the audience said that he thought
one day it would become a capital offence to kill dolphins.

The indefatigable and delightful Nan Rice escorted us to Port
Elizabeth. There we met and interviewed Anne Rennie whose experiences
with captive dolphins raised again the controversial issue of keeping
dolphins in captivity. We then flew to Durban where the Director of the
dolphinarium, Lex Fearnhead was most anxious to tell us of the scientific
work that was being carried out at the dolphinarium in addition to the
dolphin shows which were put on for the benefit of the public.

Permission was granted for me to dive with the dolphins and, kitted-up
in my wetsuit and aqualung, I joined the two Bottlenosed dolphins in the
main pool. Lex, who was equipped with just fins, mask and snorkel
followed me into the water. He emphasised how important it was to have
contact with the dolphins. Much to his surprise, Purdey, normally the
more retiring of the two female dolphins, seemed to attach herself to me,
whilst Gambit preferred the company of the Director. When I first sank to
the bottom of the pool, the dolphins circled excitedly around me. I did not
know from which direction they would come and suddenly found my leg
in a mouthful of sharp teeth. I had experienced such behaviour with
Donald in the wild and knew it was one of the ways he used for
investigating me.

Shortly before the first of the afternoon shows was due to start, I
clambered out of the main pool and visited the two Dusky dolphins who
were in an adjacent pool. Their names were Nyaluthi and Tandi. These
two dolphins were amongst the most beautiful animals I had ever seen.
Their smooth lines and shining bodies were enhanced by their colouration
which managed to be both striking and subtle at the same time. No

human artist could improve upon those two—their elegance surpassed the finest porcelain figures. Their eyes were bright and inquisitive. They signalled to me a kind of aloof detachment which seemed to imply that there was far more going on inside their minds than I as a mere human being was ever capable of understanding. I quickly discovered that their teeth were needle sharp, when they decided to nibble my arms and legs and they had no difficulty in puncturing my skin through the neoprene protection of my wetsuit. One of the trainers told

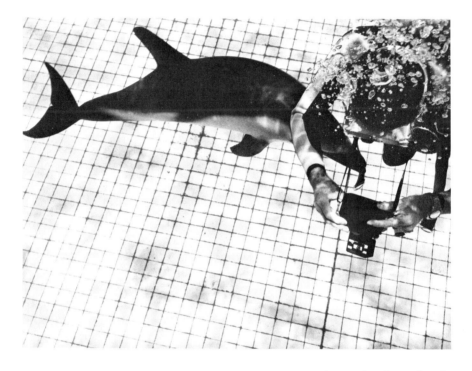

In Durban Dolphinarium the Dusky dolphin came and examined me closely, nipping me with his sharp teeth.

Lex Fearnhead.

me that he thought the Dusky dolphins were more intelligent than the Bottlenosed dolphins. It took only five minutes for these smaller, sharp-beaked dolphins to learn their tricks. When they jumped they seemed to fly through the air like swallows.

The care and attention lavished on each of the dolphins in the Durban Dolphinarium was impressive. However, there was another important ingredient in their welfare. That was the genuine affection which all of the staff, from the Director downwards, obviously had for the dolphins in their care.

I discussed the issue of keeping dolphins in captivity with Lex Fearnhead. Whilst he agreed that in an ideal situation dolphins should be free, he could see no way of conducting detailed studies on dolphins in the wild. He also made the point that the only way in which most people will ever see dolphins is in a dolphinarium. Thus he justified the capture and confinement of relatively few dolphins. He deplored the retention of dolphins in tiny unhygienic pools by travelling circuses—a situation which Nan Rice and her colleagues had done much to prevent in South Africa. However, to Nan Rice, depriving dolphins of their freedom, even under the ideal conditions of the Durban Dolphinarium, was something which she felt strongly to be morally wrong.

She was not alone in holding this view. To Kenneth le Vasseur and Steven Sipman, who worked in a dolphin laboratory in Hawaii, it became intolerable that intelligent animals should spend their lives doing thousands of repetitious tests in a tank which was so shallow they could not even dive to their eight-foot body length. They regarded the dolphins as slaves and it was from this standpoint that they chose to refer to their operation as The Undersea Railroad—deriving the name from the pre-American Civil War abolitionist slave-freeing network known as The Underground Railroad. The two men did not think of themselves as criminals when they loaded two dolphins into a foam padded truck and released them in the sea on 29 May 1977.

In the United States of America, once wild animals are caught they become the property of their owners. Le Vasseur and Sipman were charged with first degree theft, a felony carrying up to five years in jail. Le Vasseur was sentenced to six months in jail and five years probation.

The trial caused many people to focus their attention on a new concept for the first time. That concept was that humans are not alone in their rights to freedom. We do not have to go back very far in human history to a time when slaves were considered simply as 'property' by law, and those who first schemed and fought for the abolition of slavery were regarded as misguided criminals by the establishment of the day.

The driving force for the abolitionists came from a deep sense of morality at a time when some ethnic groups, such as black Africans, were considered as lower animals by many white Europeans. At the time there was what in modern speech would be termed 'no scientific evidence', to suggest otherwise. The evidence came later, when blacks and whites graduated from the same universities.

Dolphin behind bars. "What right have we to imprison these normally free-ranging animals?" was one of the questions I asked at Durban Dolphinarium.

Horace Dobbs.

Only time, and a great deal of heartsearching, will tell if a similar analogy can be drawn between men and dolphins. The problem will be a thousand times more difficult to resolve.

One person who is making a valiant attempt to find out is a New Zealander by the name of Wade Doak. A series of incidents caused Wade and his wife Jan to sell up everything that kept them tied to the land and take to the sea to study dolphins in a manner never before attempted.

On an exquisite, calm day Wade and Jan were surrounded by about thirty dolphins who lolled and gently played around the Doak's small runabout boat. Jan dived and dolphin-kicked, keeping her legs together like a dolphin's tail. One dolphin seemed to take a very special interest in Jan and stayed close by her. At the end of their session together she got the very distinct impression that the dolphins were attempting to teach her something.

'All I wanted to do was to forget everything and swim off with them,' she later reported.

Jan Doak dressed in a wet suit designed to make her overall shape more like that of a dolphin. She quickly found she could swim almost effortlessly for long periods with her legs together using a dolphin-like stroke.

Wade Doak.

'I'll never forget that one dolphin and the look in his eyes. He circled close. He was very friendly. Intelligent eye, understanding, playful, inquisitive and very, very wise, all at once. Climbing out of the water it all seemed like a dream, but it was very real. Dolphins in a wild state had come of their own free will to play with us.'

Captivated by the charm of the dolphins, Wade pondered on ways to bring himself and his family more into contact with the mysterious magnetic sea-mammals.

Eventually Project Interlock took shape and the Doaks sold their house, their car and their runabout boat, and invested in an eleven metre Polynesian sailing catamaran designed by James Wharram. Between the two hulls they slung a bow hammock which would enable them to get very

The ying-yang symbol painted on the hull of the Doak's Wharram Catamaran symbolised the link between man and dolphins.

Wade Doak.

close to dolphins in the water. Speakers were placed in each bow to transmit stereo music and a special message tape with sound frequencies used by man and dolphins. A roundel bearing the ying-yang symbol of polar opposites, with a dolphin in one and a stylised diver in the other, was specially designed by the artist Hal Chapman. Four of these roundels were fitted to the bows to symbolise the bridge between man and dolphins. It was a courageous move because the Doaks knew nothing about sailing and had no financial back-up.

Since their project got underway the Doaks have had many wonderful experiences with dolphins and continue to evolve their theories about mental telepathy between men and dolphins.

Although it would have been much easier to study dolphins in captivity, the primary tenet upon which Wade Doak based his investigations was that the dolphins should be *free* in the sea. Kenneth le Vasseur and Steven Sipman set out deliberately to set dolphins *free*. Nan Rice and her colleagues worked to prevent the capture of dolphins and used the slogan 'Dolphins should be *free*'.

I came to the conclusion that the key to the human–dolphin connection I was searching for was freedom; not just physical freedom, but the *spirit of freedom* that is present in both man and dolphins and may be endowed because of their large brains.

Looking back at all of my experiences with Donald I feel intuitively that it was a common spirit of freedom that brought us together. I cannot prove it—I just sense it.

I find myself attracted by people who have the equivalent quality in human terms. It finds expression in many different ways—often as a kind of non-violent rebelliousness against the rules of a society that is becoming too ordered. In some cases it is the force that ultimately compels them to sell up everything and sail round the world.

In their attempts to probe this human dolphin link in Project Interlock, the Doaks approached dolphins as they would nomadic tribesmen with an alien culture. This is an interesting analogy as in the broadest sense primitive people have also been regarded as cousins to the white man. The basis for the analogy between dolphins and nomadic tribesmen can be appreciated when one considers the way of life of the nomadic aborigines of Australasia before the intrusion of white colonialists.

The aborigines did not dominate the land but became an integral part of it. They mastered the use of fire but did not manufacture metal. Their ability to create and use tools did not extend beyond the simplest modification of the sticks and bones they found around them into weapons for hunting. Spiritual and visual images (what we would call art) played an important part in their lives. To such people, whose passage through life was part of a continuum of spiritual existence, possessions were an impediment. Over a period of 400,000 years complex cultures were developed which were passed from generation to generation without the use of a written language.

Man's exploration, exploitation and understanding of the sea has now reached a stage equivalent to that of the voyages of discovery that led to the colonisation of the hitherto remote and uncivilised major land masses of the world more than a century ago. By reviewing what became of the aborigines of Australia and Tasmania, and again applying the analogy

A man with a dream. Wade Doak gave up a secure job and sold most of his possessions in order that he and his family could interlock with wild dolphins. From the mail I receive I know there are hundreds with similar visions. But there are only a handful in the entire world who have had the courage to do so.

Estelle Myers.

between man and dolphins, we can take a lesson from history that should influence our attitude and future treatment of our cousins in the sea.

A report by Susan Raven in the Sunday Times Magazine (21 May 1978) included a horrifying account of how the Stone Age survivors of Tasmania were hunted to extinction by the white settlers.

'It is a sorry history—backed by guns—of murder and rape; of Sunday afternoon man-hunts; of indescribable tortures. An aboriginal baby was buried up to its neck in sand, and its head was kicked off in front of its mother. A woman, repeatedly raped, was made to wear round her neck the severed head of her husband. There were stories of flesh being cut from the bodies of living men and fed to the dogs.'

The last true Tasmanian died on 8 May 1876. One hundred years later, her skeleton, which had been on display in the Hobart museum, was truly laid to rest. It was cremated and the ashes were scattered on the sea—the same sea which had carried white men hunting for seals bringing with them guns and death.

The aborigines of Australia were treated with no more understanding or tolerance by the British who were transported to a new continent. Unlike their Tasmanian counterparts, however, some of the Australian aborigines were able to escape extinction by virtue of the sheer size and inhospitable nature of the sunburnt Never-Never land into which they dissolved like sugar in tea.

To a people who did not evolve through a civilisation based on acquisitions and wealth, the arrival of the whites was bemusing. To the aborigines, for whom possessions were encumbrances that obstructed rather than aided their long walk through life, whose stories were written in the stones of the hills and for whom the spirits were all important, the invasion by the land-grabbers was a destructive force which they could neither understand nor combat. Those who survived found their way of life destroyed. In exchange for a free existence in a land which they inherited but did not own, they were awarded a few paltry possessions, second class citizenship in an acquisitive society, and the solace of alcohol.

It does not stretch the imagination too far to relate what has happened in the past to the aborigines to what is happening and will happen to the dolphins in the future. With their capacity for memory and their large cerebral cortexes, it is conceivable that the dolphins have a submarine culture that is as complex and even more deep-rooted than that of the aborigines. The value of the heritage of the dolphins (if it exists) or the culture of the aborigines cannot be measured in our terms—the beauty of a tree cannot be measured with a ruler. To comprehend it we must find a new set of values based on tolerance and freedom. If we can do that we will do more than save some fellow creatures from extinction.

THE END